Piano • Vocal • Guitar

MIDNIGHT OIL
20,000 WATT R.S.L.

ISBN 978-1-4950-9623-5

HAL•LEONARD®
7777 W. BLUEMOUND RD. P.O. BOX 13819 MILWAUKEE, WI 53213

In Australia Contact:
Hal Leonard Australia Pty. Ltd.
4 Lentara Court
Cheltenham, Victoria, 3192 Australia
Email: ausadmin@halleonard.com.au

Visit Hal Leonard Online at
www.halleonard.com

WHAT GOES ON

Words and Music by ROBERT HIRST
and JAMES MOGINIE

Industrial Rock

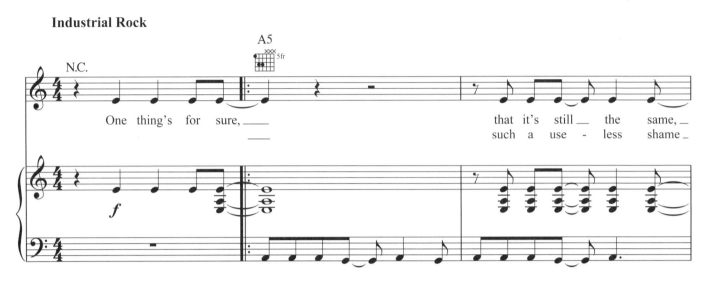

One thing's for sure, _____ that it's still _____ the same, _____
_____ such a use - less shame _____

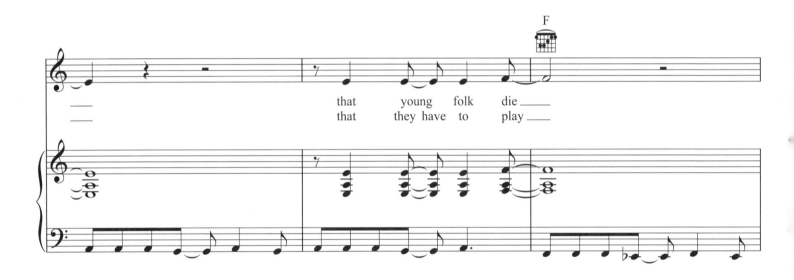

_____ that young folk die _____
_____ that they have to play _____

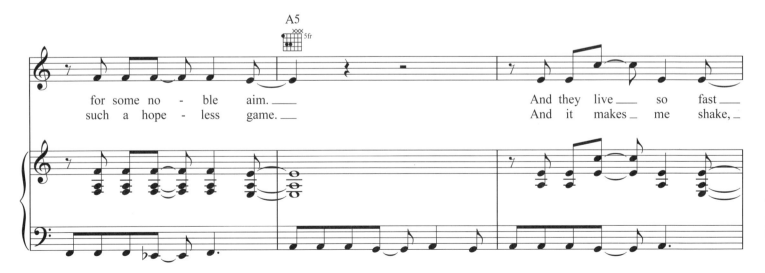

for some no - ble aim. _____ And they live _____ so fast
such a hope - less game. _____ And it makes _____ me shake,

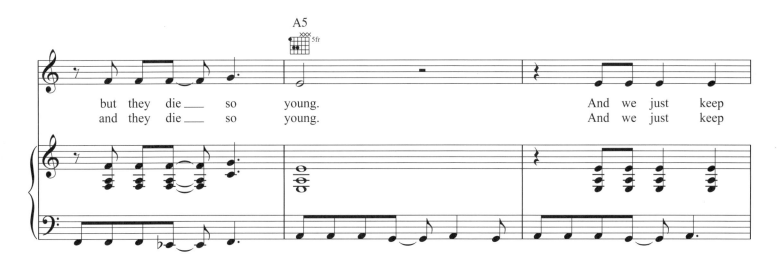

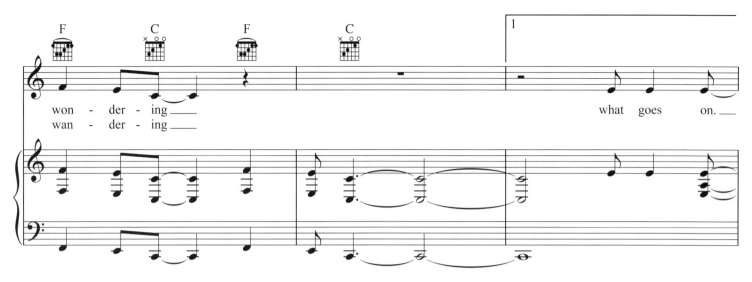

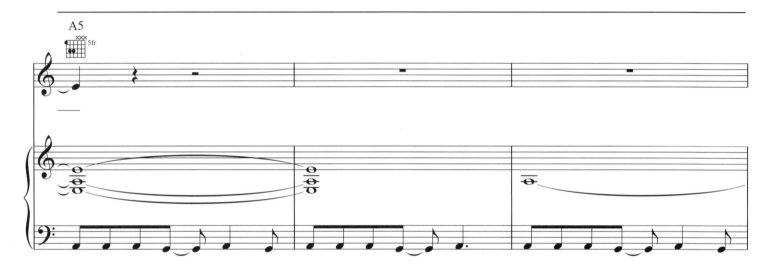

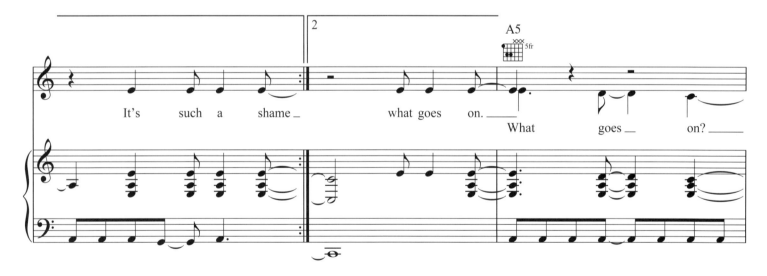

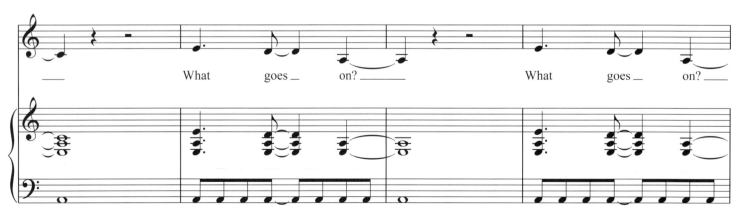

You tell me, what goes ___ on? ___ What goes ___ on? _____

What goes ___ on? _____

You got a good thing be -

fore. You got ev - 'ry-thing to live for.

Ain't noth-ing you want to die ___ for. No, ___ no, no-thing at

all. 'Cause you live ___ so fast ___

but you die ___ so young. And we just ___ keep

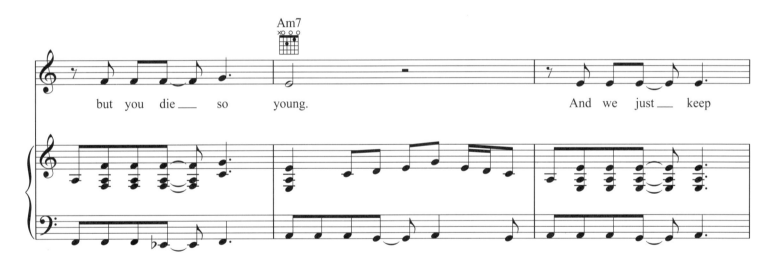

won - der - ing, ___ won - der - ing...

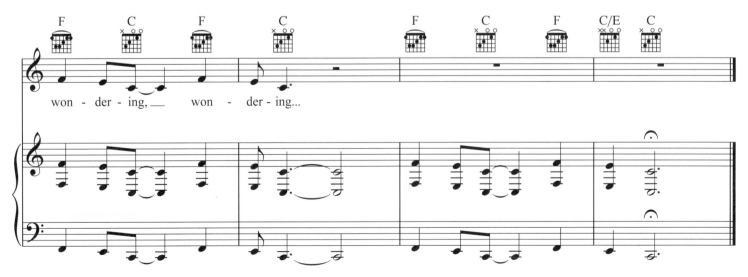

DREAMWORLD

Words and Music by JAMES MOGINIE,
PETER GARRETT and ROBERT HIRST

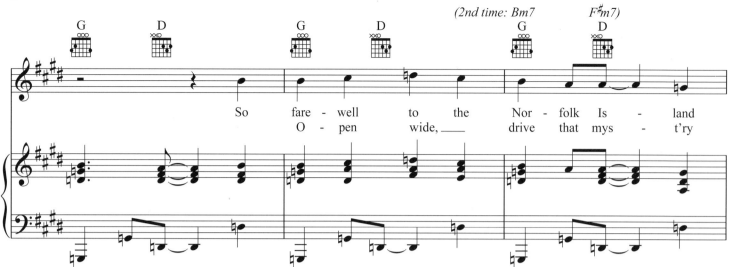

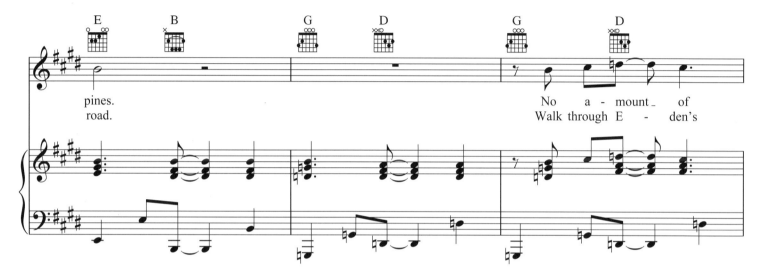

(End.) _____

(Fall.) _____

Your dream-world is just a-bout_ to fall. _____

Your dream-world will fall.

So

Your dream - world is just a - bout ___ to fall. ___

Sign says, "Hon-ey-moon to rent." _____

Cloud-land in - to dream - land turns.

The sun comes up and we all learn, _____ those

wheels must _ turn. _____

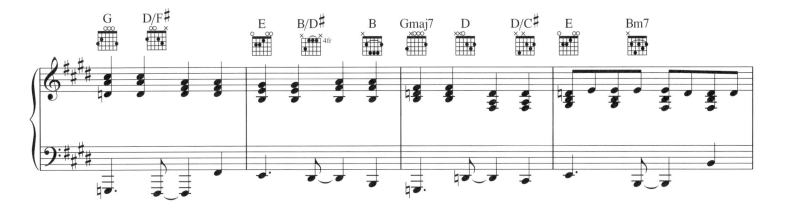

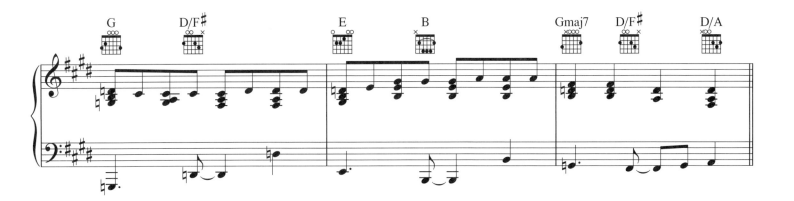

(End.) _____ Your dream - world is

just a - bout ___ to end. _____

(Fall.) _____ Your dream - world is

just a - bout ___ to fall. _____

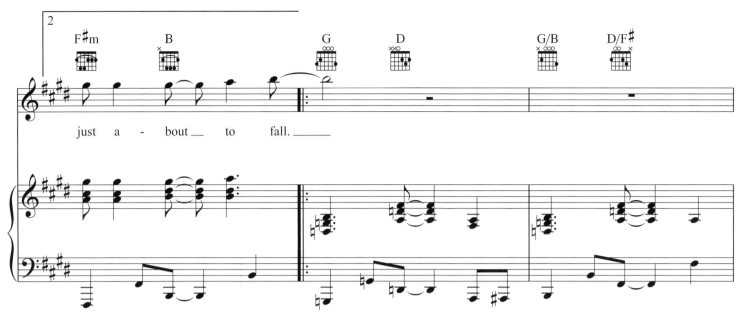

just a - bout __ to fall. _____

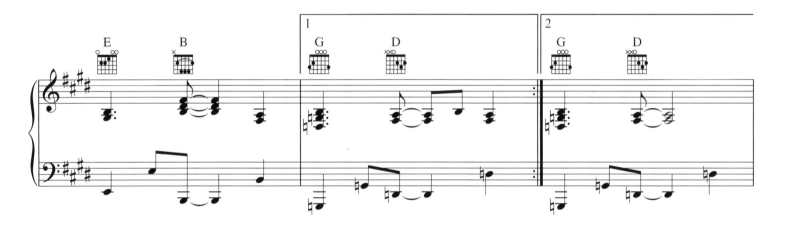

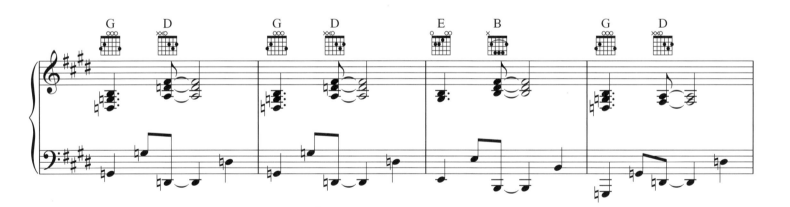

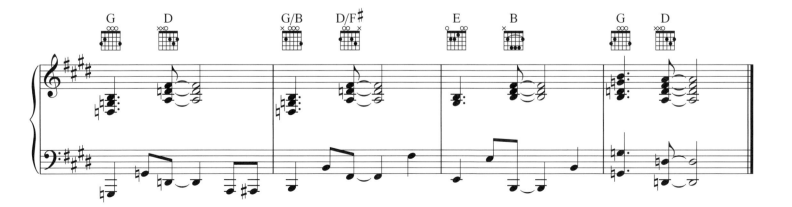

POWER AND THE PASSION

Words and Music by ROBERT HIRST,
JAMES MOGINIE and PETER GARRETT

Moderate Rock

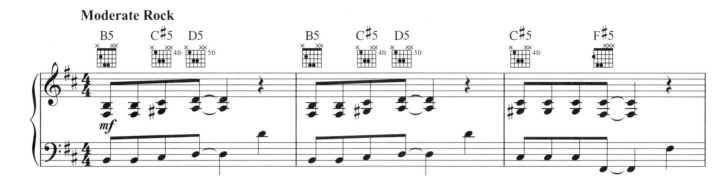

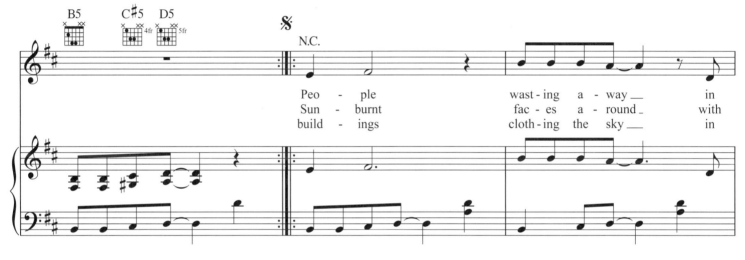

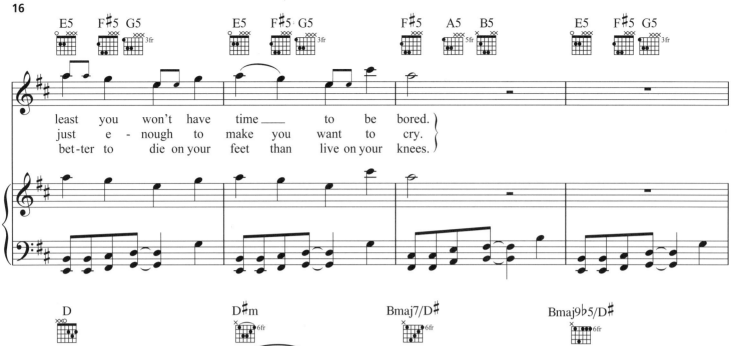

least you won't have time ___ to be bored.
just e - nough to make you want to cry.
bet-ter to die on your feet than live on your knees.

Oh, ___ the pow - er and the pas - sion. ___

(Chord 2nd x only.
All others are percussion only.)

Oh, ___ the tem - per of the time.

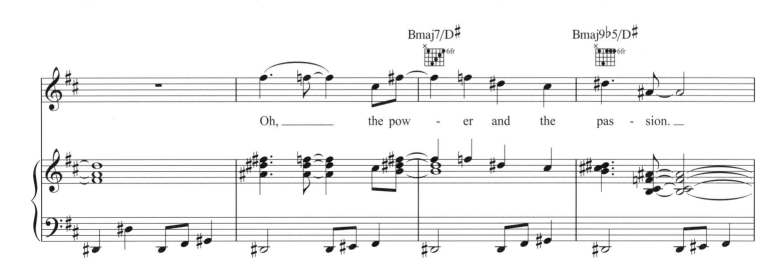

Oh, ___ the pow - er and the pas - sion. ___

18

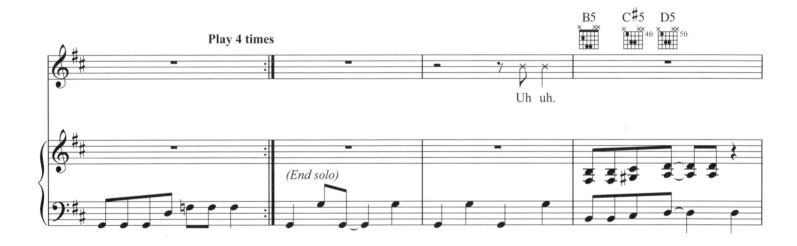

CODA

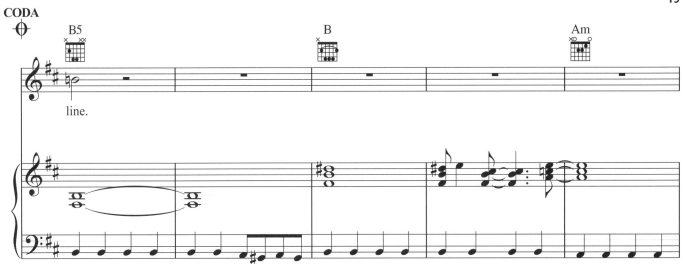

line.

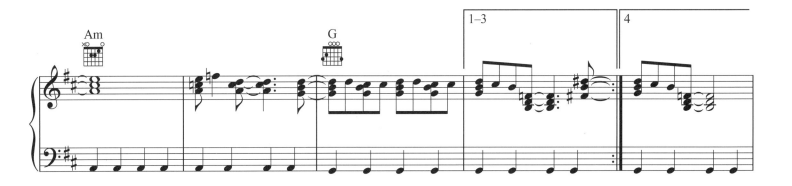

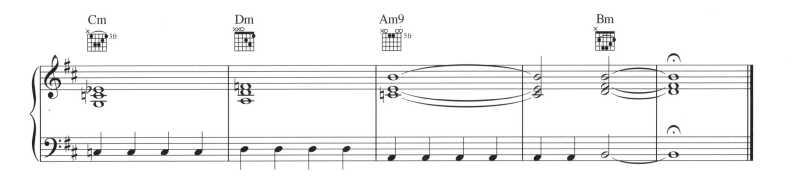

WHITE SKIN BLACK HEART

Words and Music by JAMES MOGINIE,
ROBERT HIRST and PETER GARRETT

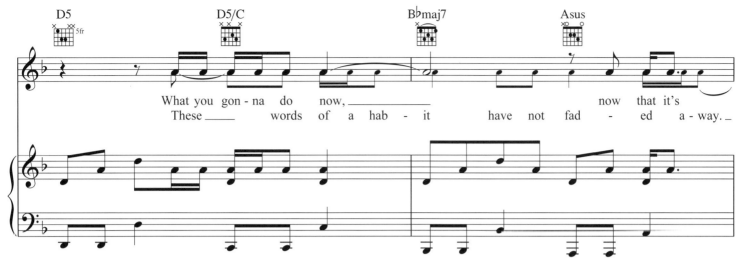

What you gon - na do now, _____ now that it's
These _____ words of a hab - it have not fad - ed a - way. _

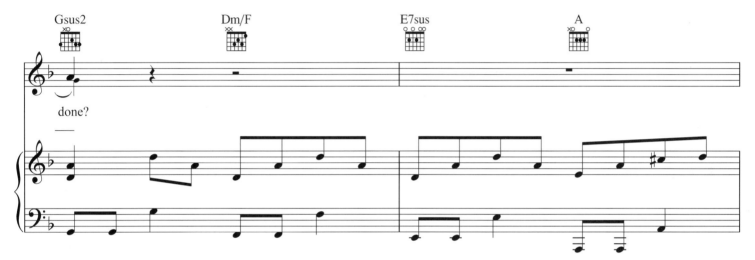

done?

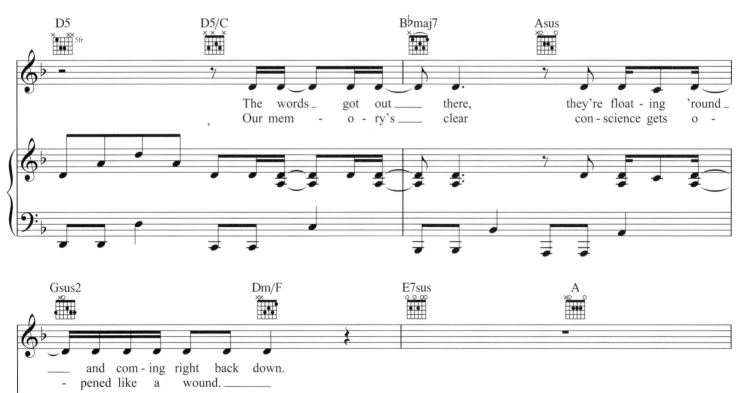

The words _ got out _____ there, they're float - ing 'round _
Our mem - o - ry's _____ clear con - science gets o -

_____ and com - ing right back down.
- pened like a wound. _____

White skin, black heart. _

Spoken: "You see the Boston Strangler

on the freedom road. You think the suffragettes got sunk a long, long time ago. You spewed it out your spite was

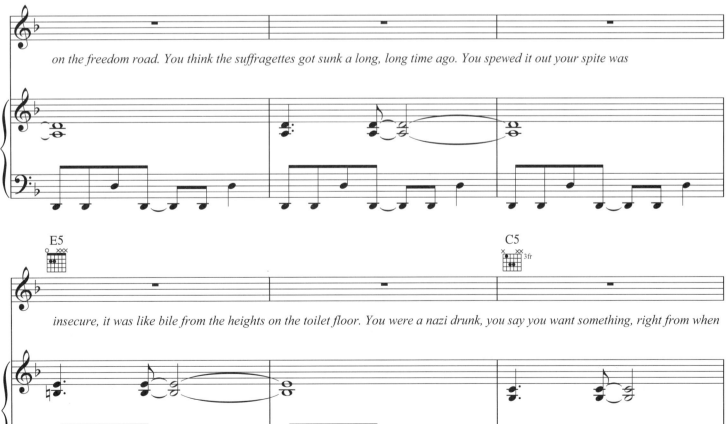

insecure, it was like bile from the heights on the toilet floor. You were a nazi drunk, you say you want something, right from when

had the rednecks roaring for blood and then they wanted more. Your life was so small you couldn't get enough, you made a start..."

2nd time: Drip - ping.   *Sing both times:* White   skin, black   heart. _

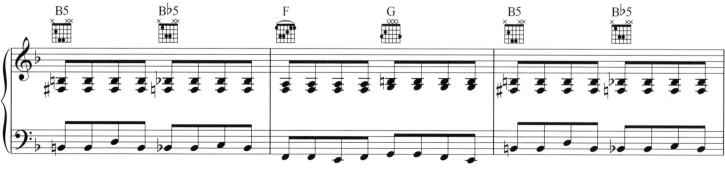

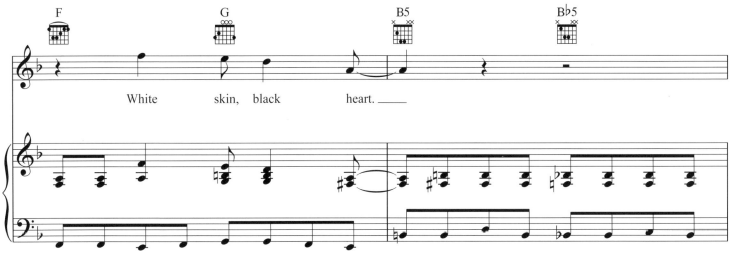

White skin, black heart. _____

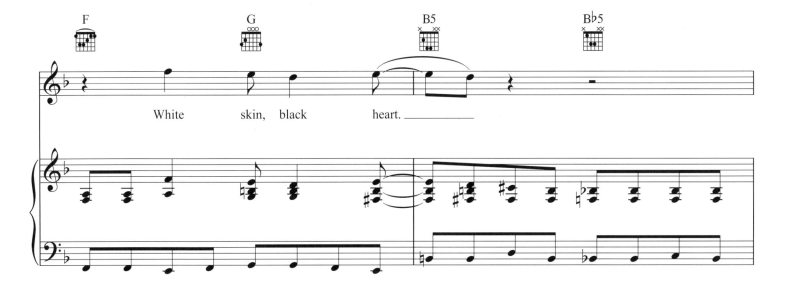

White skin, black heart. _____

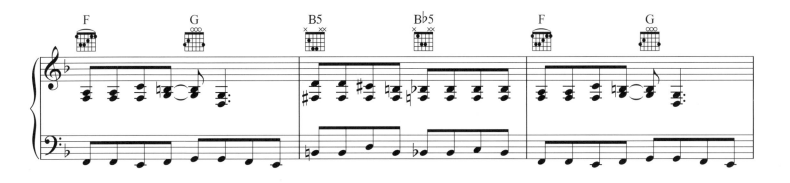

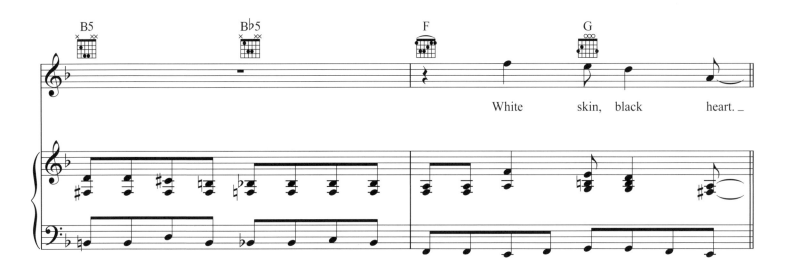

White skin, black heart. _

BLUE SKY MINE

Words and Music by JAMES MOGINIE,
Peter Garrett, ROBERT HIRST,
MARTIN ROTSEY and WAYNE STEVENS

Driving Rock beat

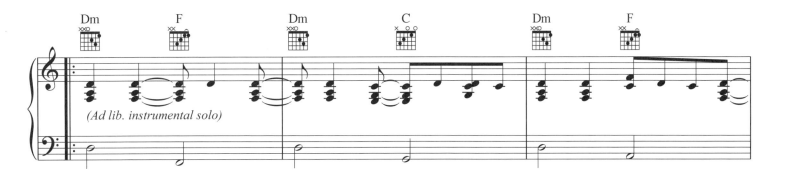

(Ad lib. instrumental solo)

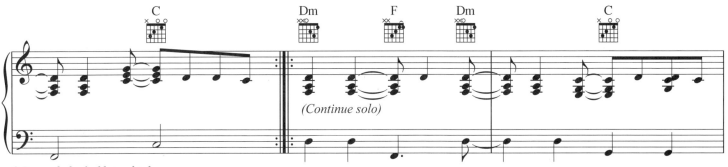

(Continue solo)

* *Recorded a half step higher.*

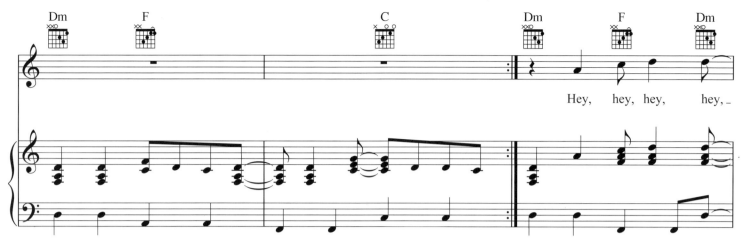

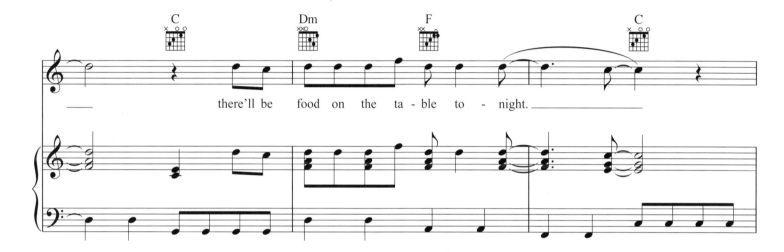

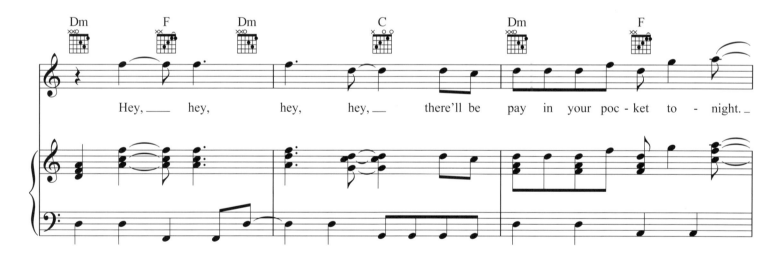

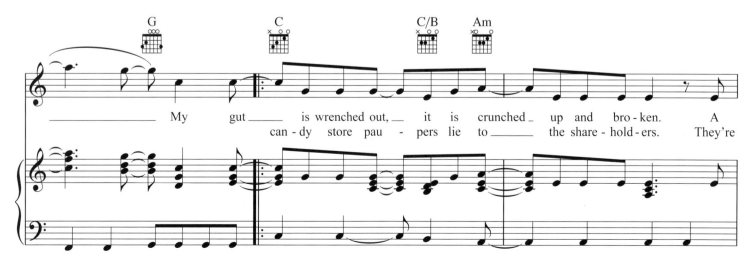

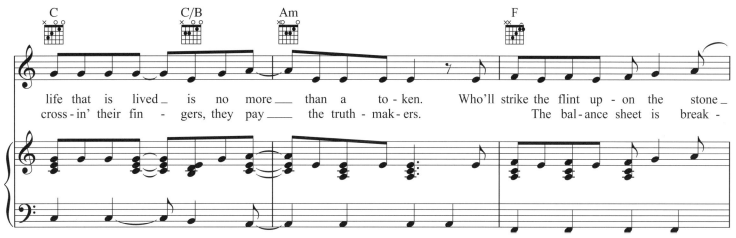

life that is lived ___ is no more ___ than a to - ken. Who'll strike the flint up - on the stone ___
cross - in' their fin - gers, they pay ___ the truth - mak - ers. The bal - ance sheet is break -

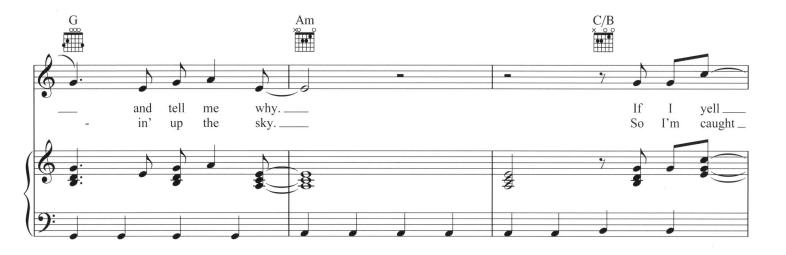

___ and tell me why. ___ If I yell ___
- in' up the sky. ___ So I'm caught ___

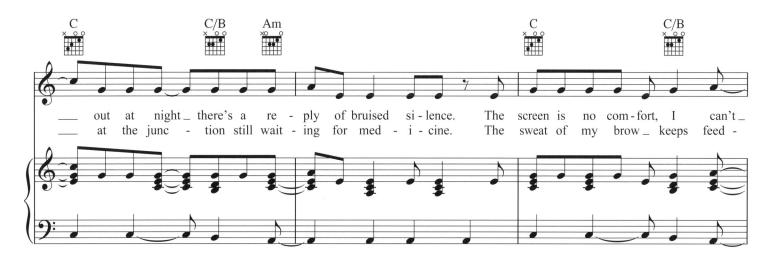

___ out at night ___ there's a re - ply of bruised si - lence. The screen is no com - fort, I can't ___
___ at the junc - tion still wait - ing for med - i - cine. The sweat of my brow ___ keeps feed -

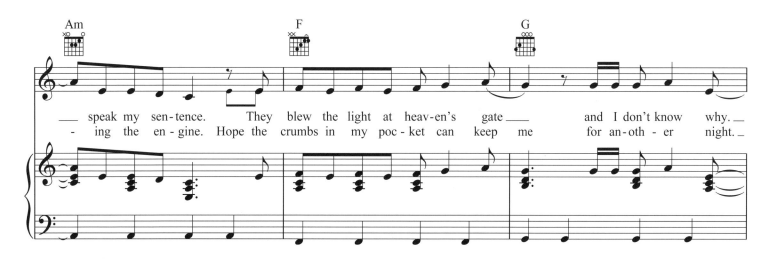

___ speak my sen - tence. They blew the light at heav - en's gate ___ and I don't know why. ___
- ing the en - gine. Hope the crumbs in my poc - ket can keep me for an - oth - er night. ___

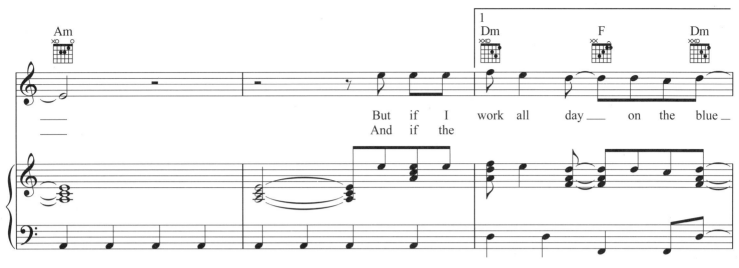

But if I work all day ___ on the blue ___
And if the

___ sky mine, ___ there'll be food on the ta - ble to - night. ___ Still I
And if I

walk up and down ___ on the blue ___ sky mine. ___ There'll be pay in your poc - ket to - night.

The blue sky min - ing com - pan - y ___ won't come ___

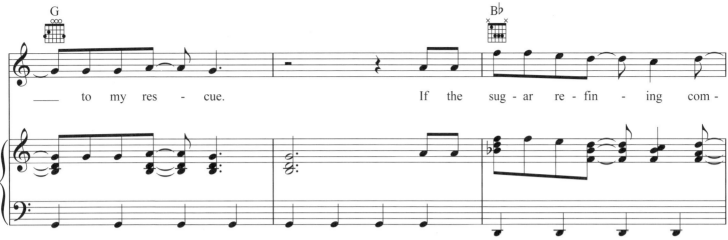

to my res - cue. If the sug - ar re - fin - ing com -

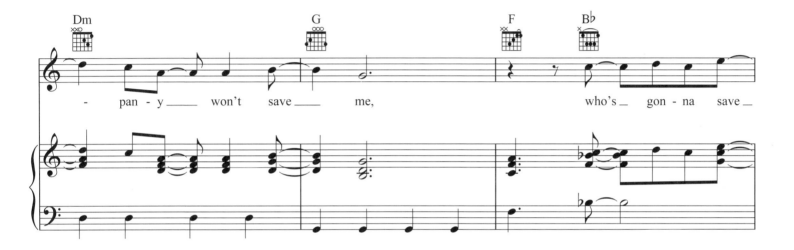

- pan - y won't save me, who's gon - na save

me? Who's gon - na save me?

Who's gon - na save me? But if I

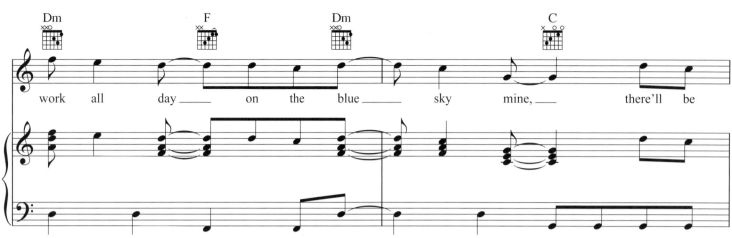

work all day ____ on the blue ____ sky mine, ____ there'll be

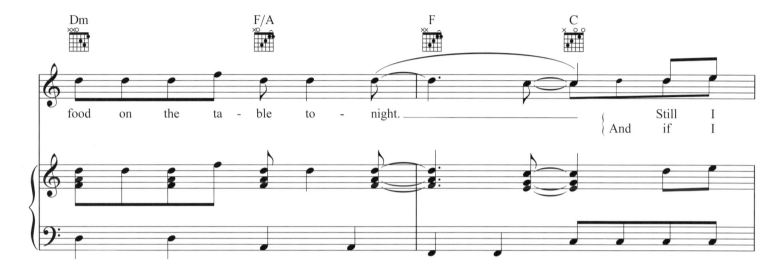

food on the ta - ble to - night. _____ { Still I
                                                 { And if I

walk up and down ____ on the blue ____ sky mine. ____ There'll be

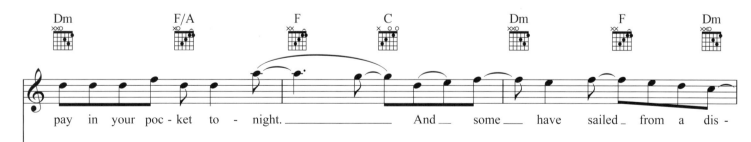

pay in your poc - ket to - night. _____ And ___ some ___ have sailed ___ from a dis -

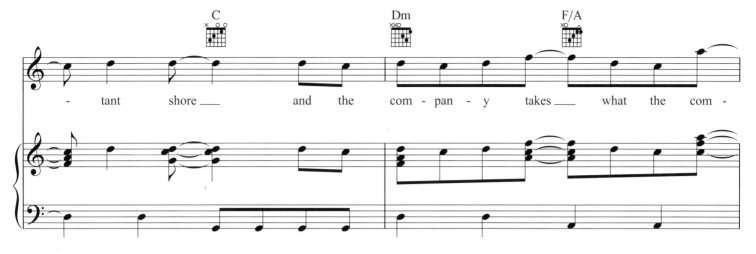

- tant shore ____ and the com - pan - y takes ____ what the com -

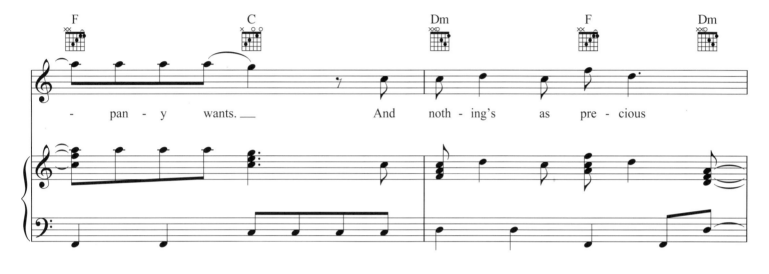

- pan - y wants. ____ And noth - ing's as pre - cious

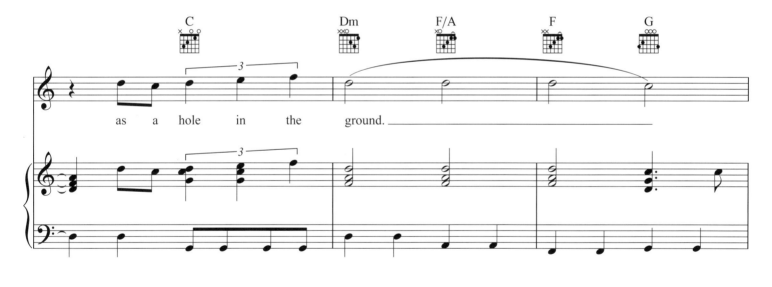

as a hole in the ground. ____

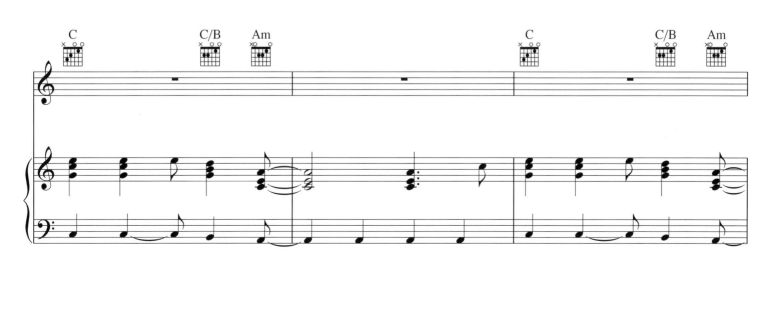

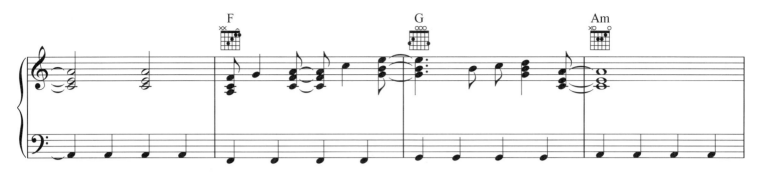

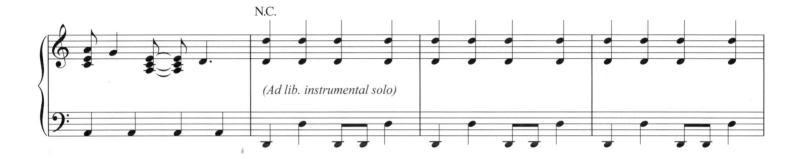

(Ad lib. instrumental solo)

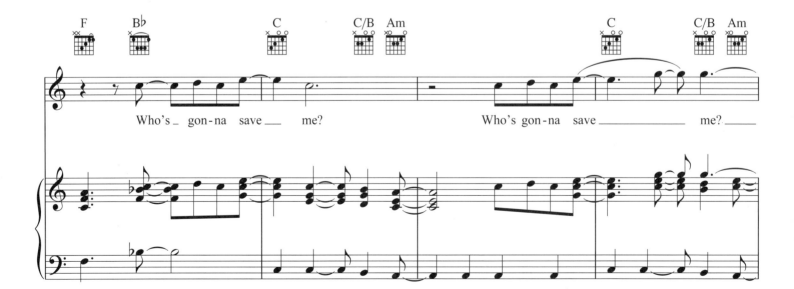

Who's _ gon-na save _ me? Who's gon-na save _____ me? ___

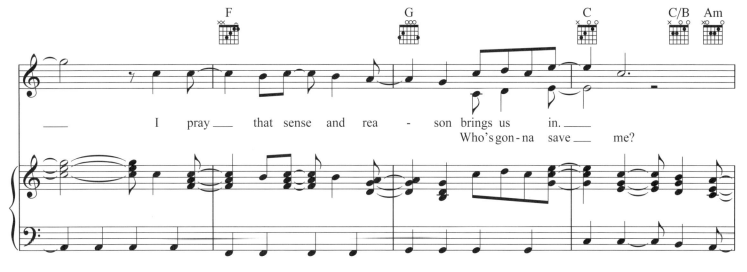

KOSCIUSZKO

Words and Music by ROBERT HIRST
and JAMES MOGINIE

Driving Rock beat

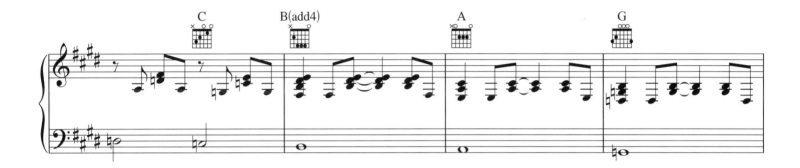

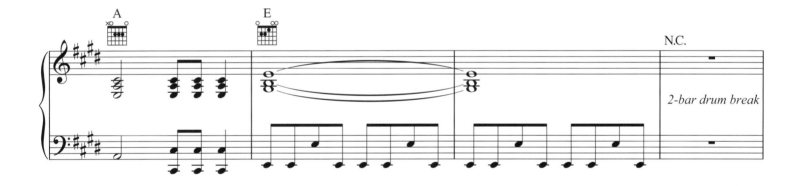

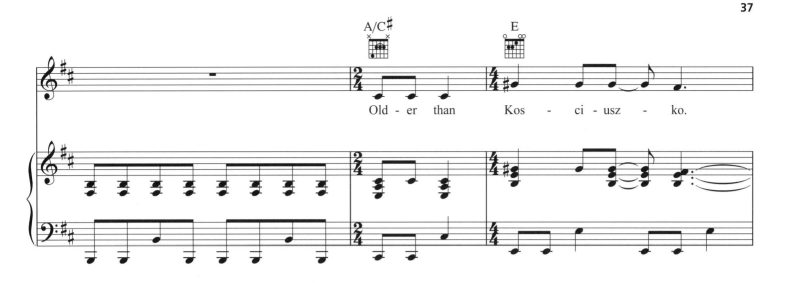

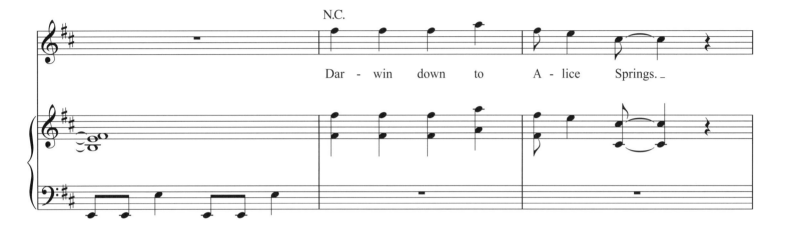

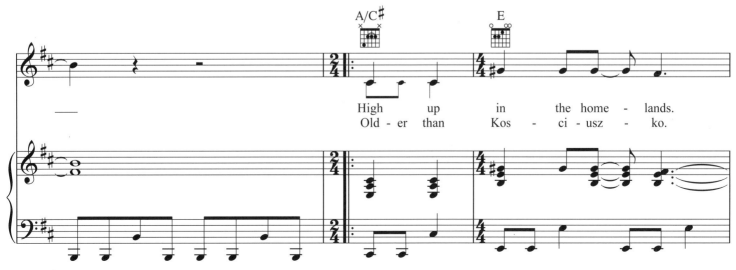

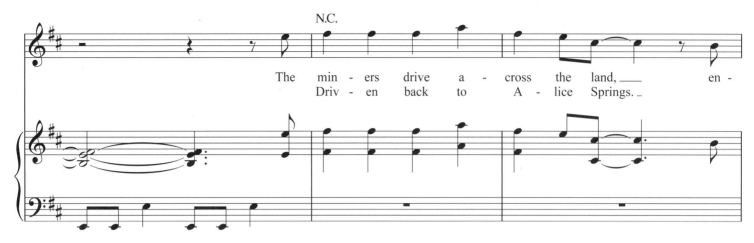

The min-ers drive a-cross the land, ___ en-
Driv-en back to A-lice Springs. _

coun-ter no re-sis-tance when the peo-ple block the road. _
End-less storms and strug-gle marks the spir-it of the age. _

Old-er than Kos-ci-usz-ko.
High _ up in the home-lands.

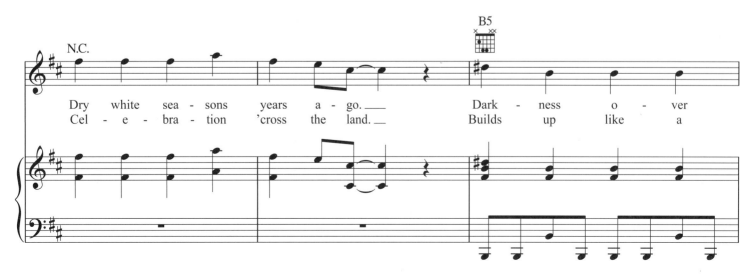

Dry white sea-sons years a-go. _ Dark-ness o-ver
Cel-e-bra-tion 'cross the land. _ Builds up like a

Char - le - ville, _ the fires _ be - gin _ to grow. _
cy - clone, now _ the fires _ be - gin _ to rage. _

No

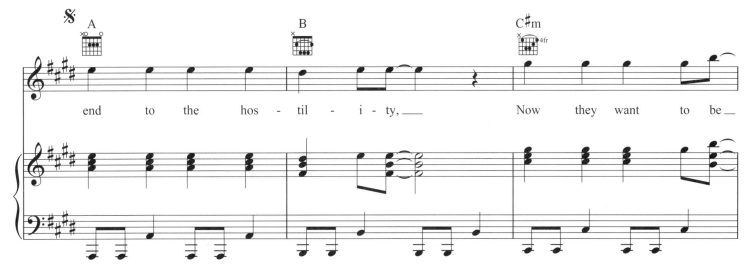

A B C#m

end to the hos - til - i - ty, _ Now they want to be _

E D D/E

_ some - where _ else. _

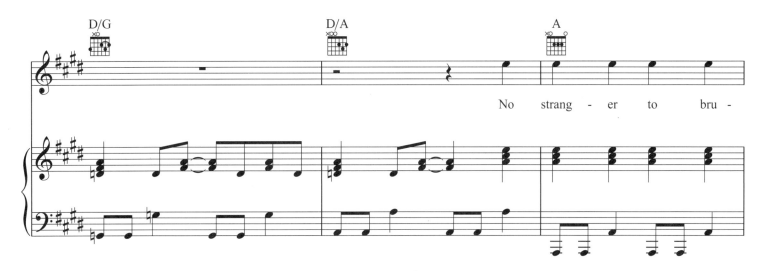

D/G D/A A

No strang - er to bru -

ta - li - ty, ___ now they'd like to be ___ some - one ___

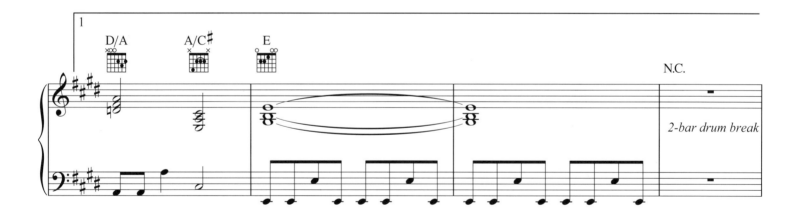

else. _

To Coda ⊕

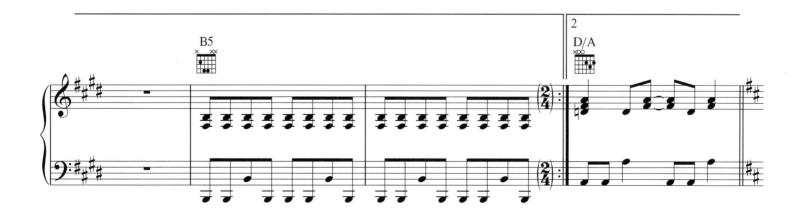

2-bar drum break

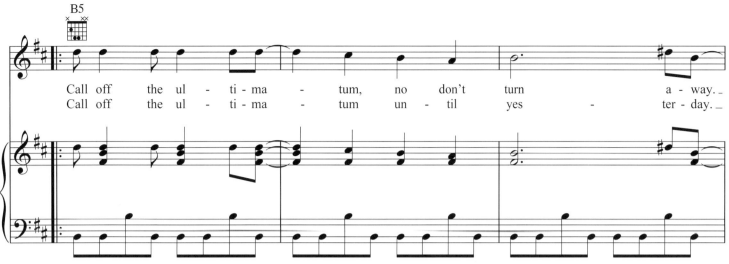

Call off the ul - ti - ma - tum, no don't turn a - way.
Call off the ul - ti - ma - tum un - til yes - ter - day.

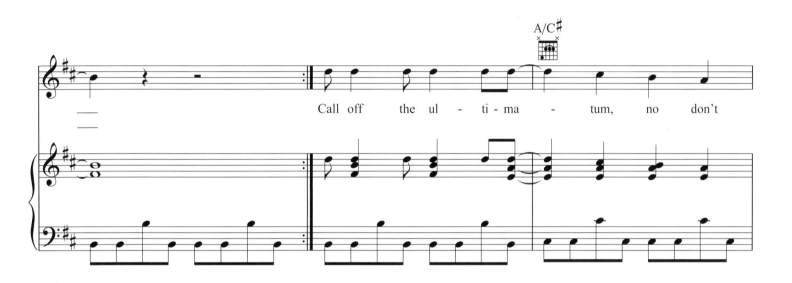

Call off the ul - ti - ma - tum, no don't

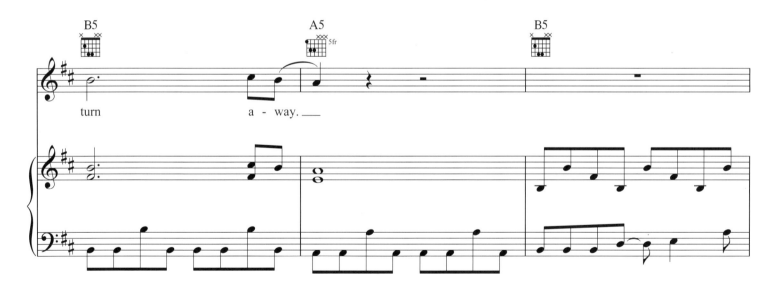

turn a - way.

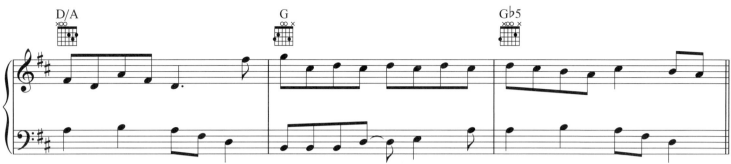

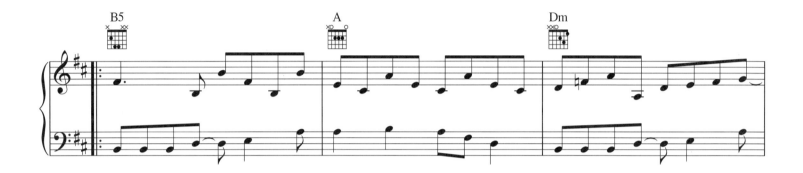

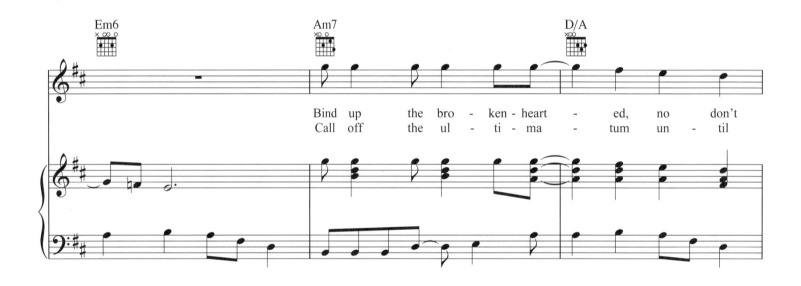

Bind up the bro - ken - heart - ed, no don't
Call off the ul - ti - ma - tum un - til

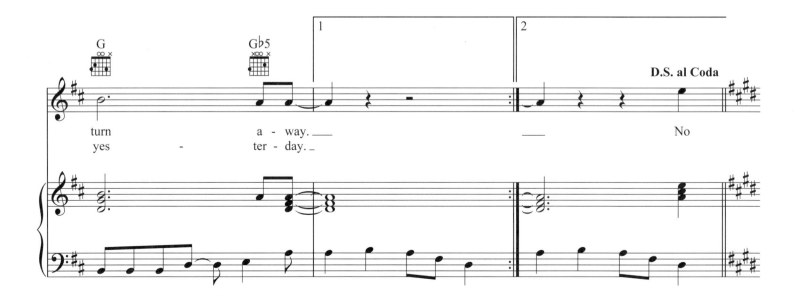

turn a - way. ___
yes - ter - day. ___

No

CODA

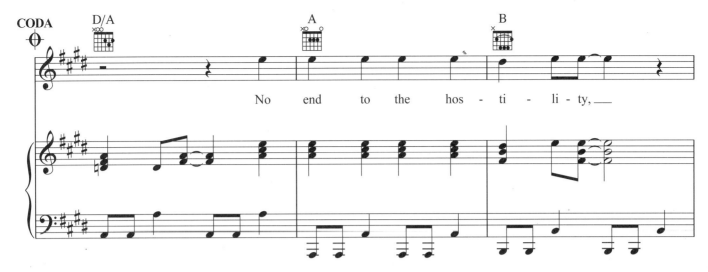

No end to the hos - ti - li - ty, ___

now they want to be ___ some - where.

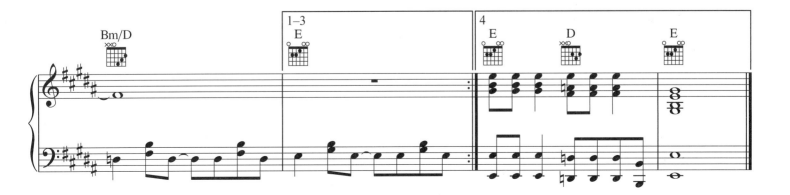

THE DEAD HEART

Words and Music by ROBERT HIRST,
JAMES MOGINIE and PETER GARRETT

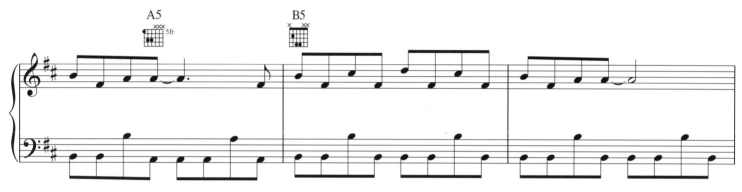

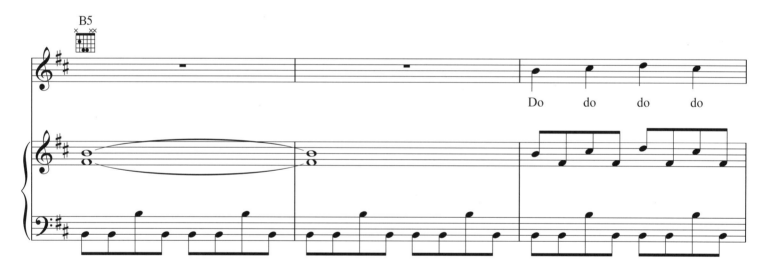

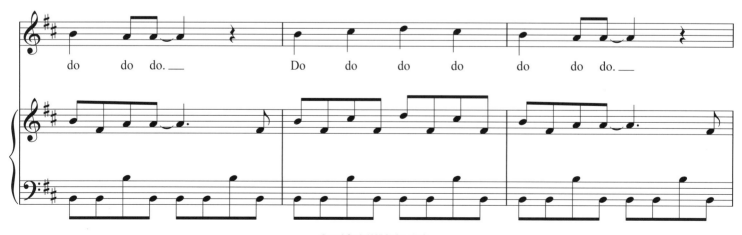

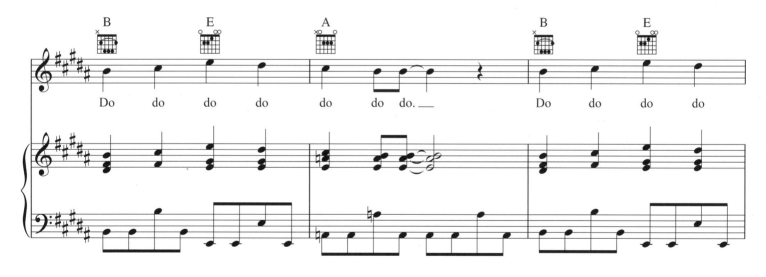

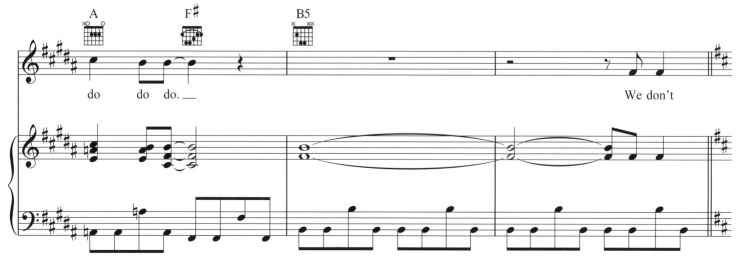

serve your coun-try, don't serve your king, _ know your cus-tom, don't
serve your coun-try, don't serve your king, _ white man lis-ten to the

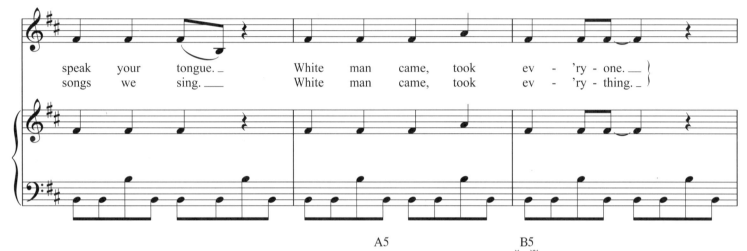

speak your tongue. _ White man came, took ev-'ry-one. _
songs we sing. _ White man came, took ev-'ry-thing. _

Do do do do do do do. _ Do do do do

do do do. _ We don't do do do. _ We

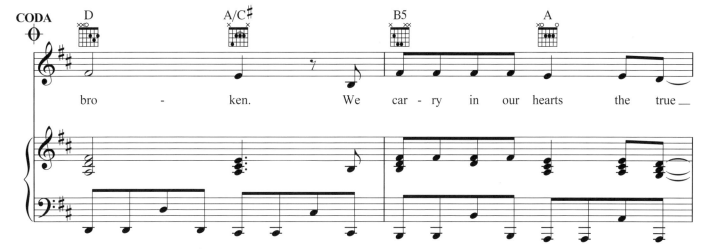

broken. We car-ry in our hearts the true

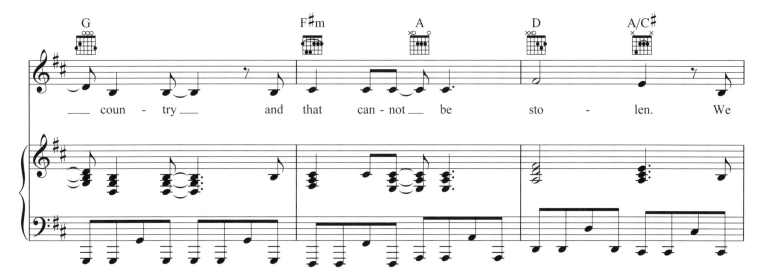

country and that can-not be sto-len. We

fol-low in the steps of our an-ces-try and

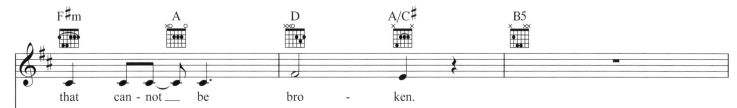

that can-not be bro-ken.

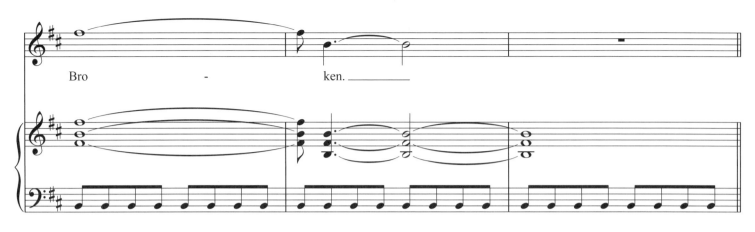

Bro - ken. _____

Do do do do do do do. _____ Do do do do

do do do. _____ Do do do do do do do. _____

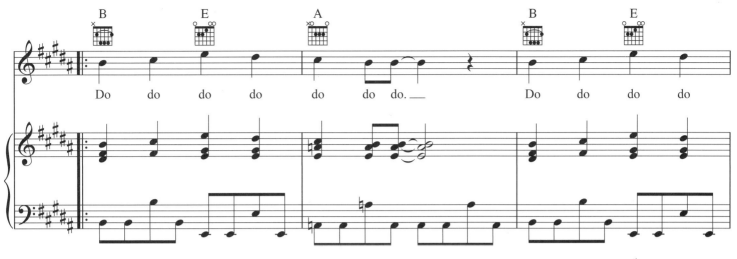

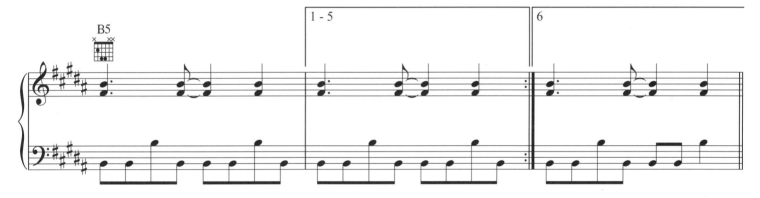

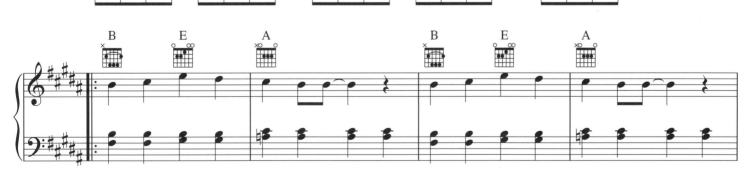

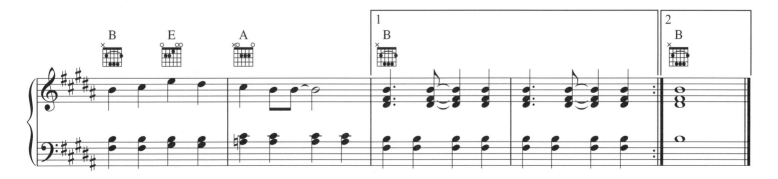

US FORCES

Words and Music by JAMES MOGINIE
and PETER GARRETT

In a steady four

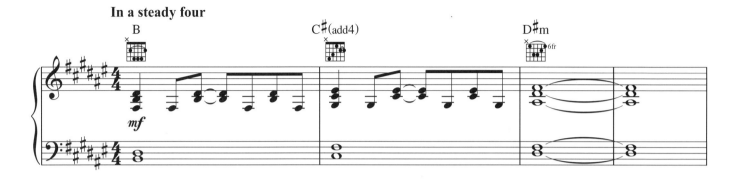

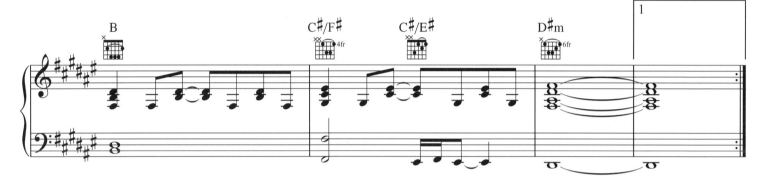

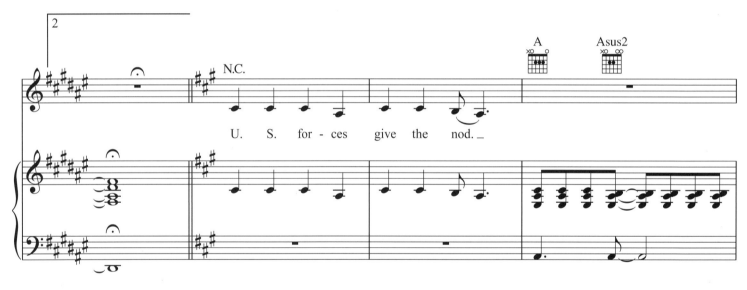

U. S. for-ces give the nod.—

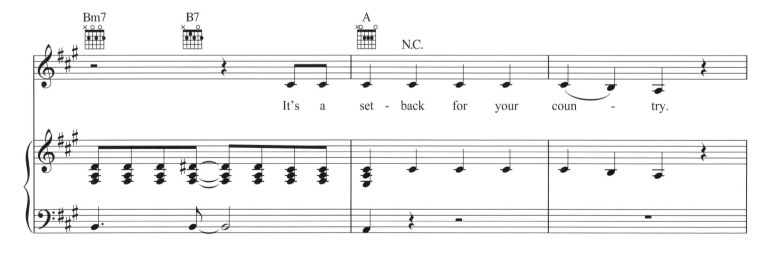

It's a set-back for your coun-try.

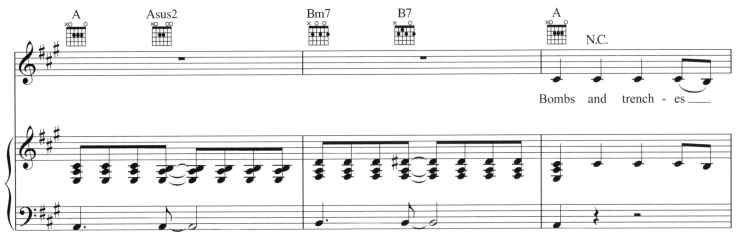

Bombs and trench-es ___

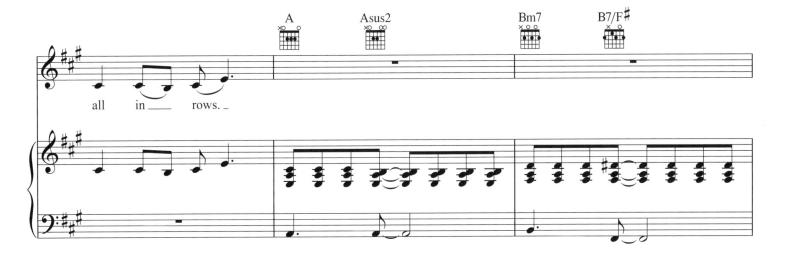

all in ___ rows. _

Bombs and threats still ask for more.

Di - vid - ed world, the C. I. A. ___

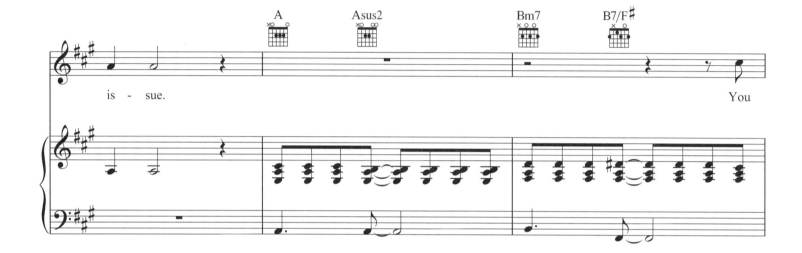

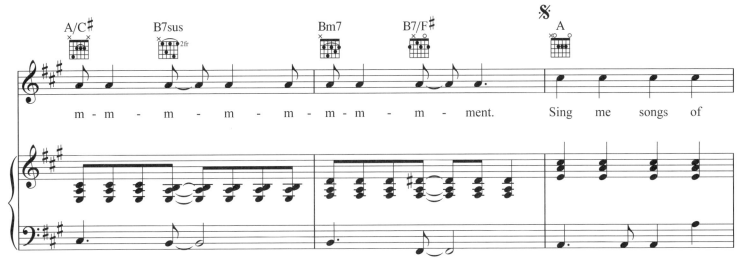

m-m-m-m-m-m-m-m-m-m-ment. Sing me songs of

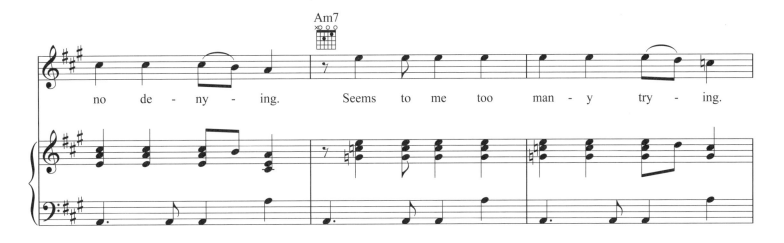

no de-ny-ing. Seems to me too man-y try-ing.

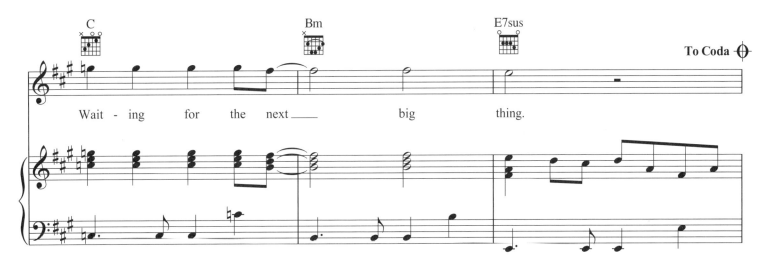

Wait-ing for the next ___ big thing.

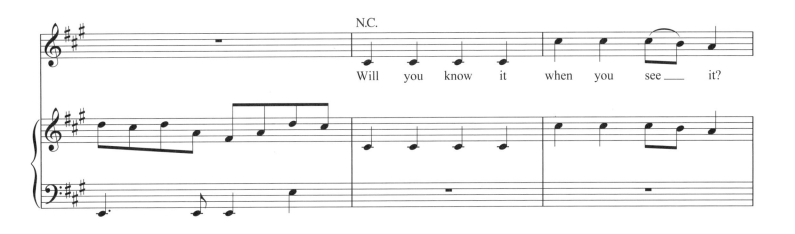

Will you know it when you see ___ it?

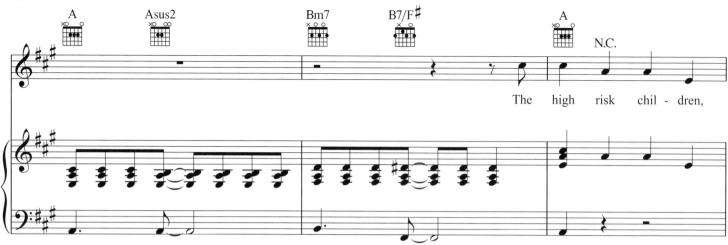

The high risk chil - dren,

dogs of ___ war.   Now

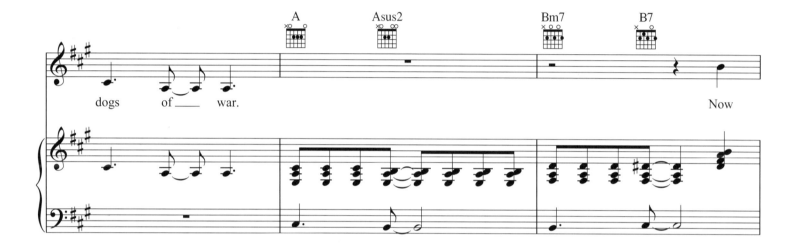

mar - ket move - ments call the shots. _ Busi - ness deals in park - ing lots. _

D.S. al Coda

Wait - ing for the meat of to - mor - row.

CODA

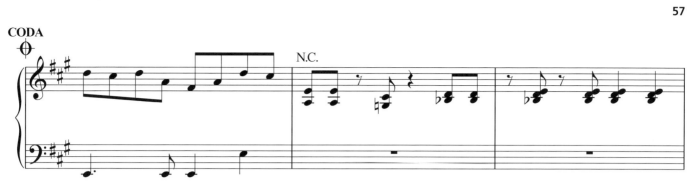

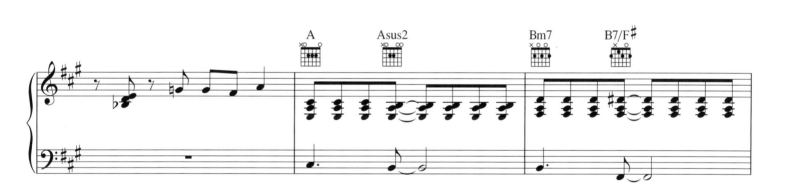

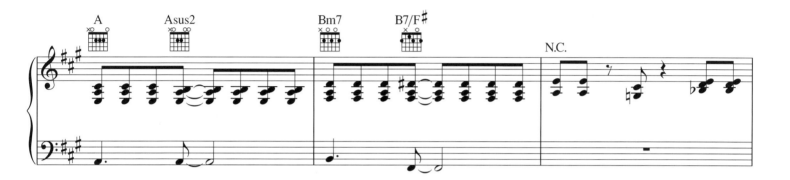

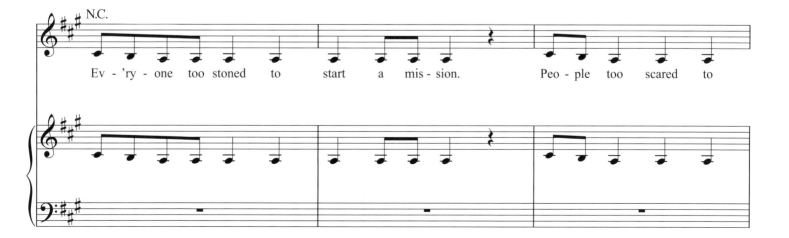

Ev - 'ry - one too stoned to start a mis - sion. Peo - ple too scared to

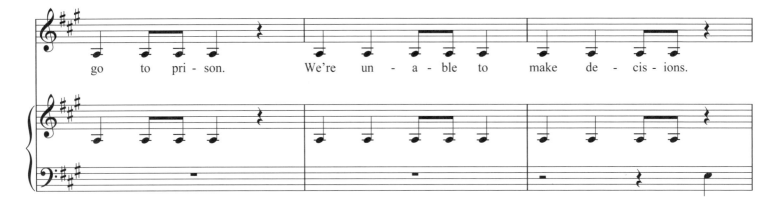

go to pri - son. We're un - a - ble to make de - cis - ions.

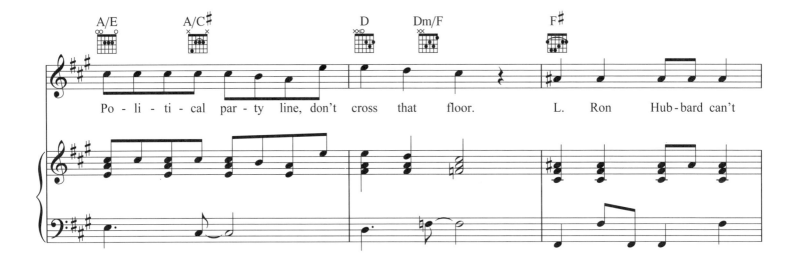

Po - li - ti - cal par - ty line, don't cross that floor. L. Ron Hub - bard can't

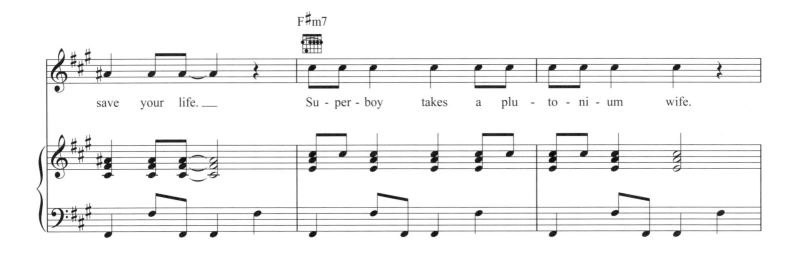

save your life. __ Su - per - boy takes a plu - to - ni - um wife.

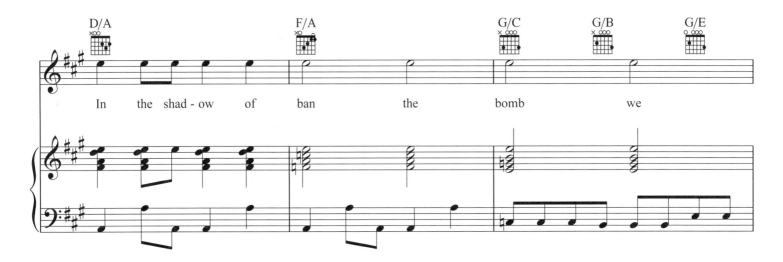

In the shad - ow of ban the bomb we

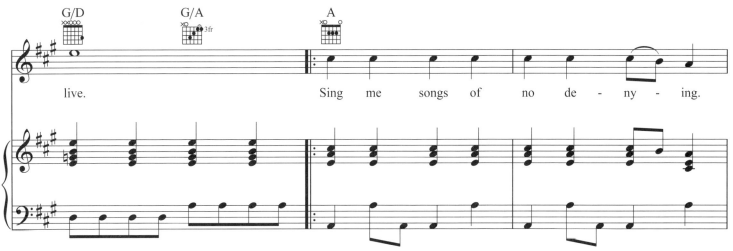

live. Sing me songs of no de - ny - ing.

Seems to me too man - y try - ing. Wait - ing for the next

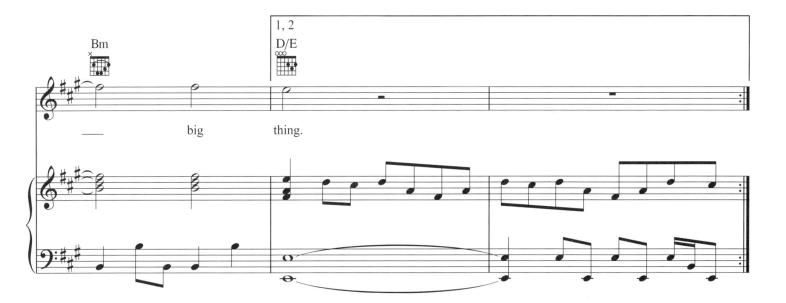

big thing.

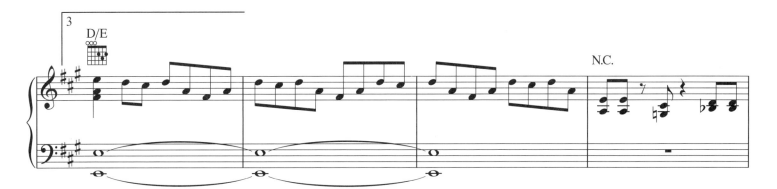

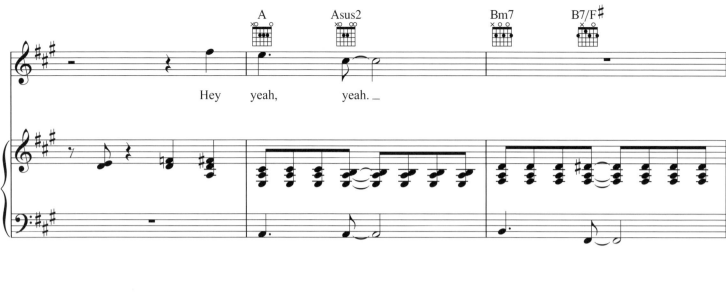

Hey yeah, yeah. _

Hey yeah, yeah. _

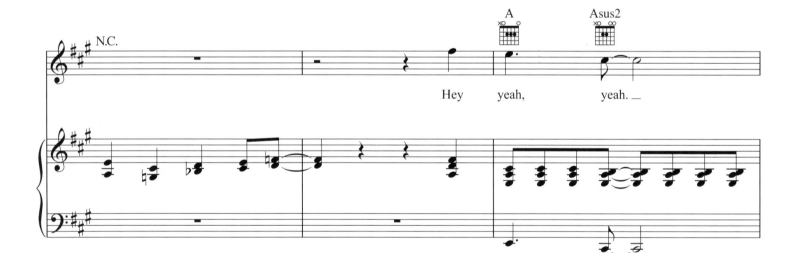

Hey yeah, yeah. _

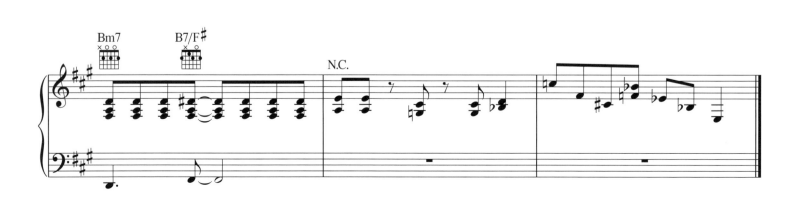

BEDS ARE BURNING

Words and Music by ROBERT HIRST,
JAMES MOGINIE and PETER GARRETT

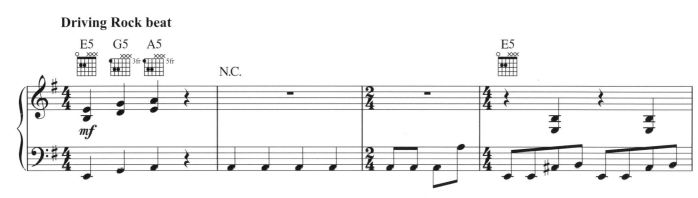

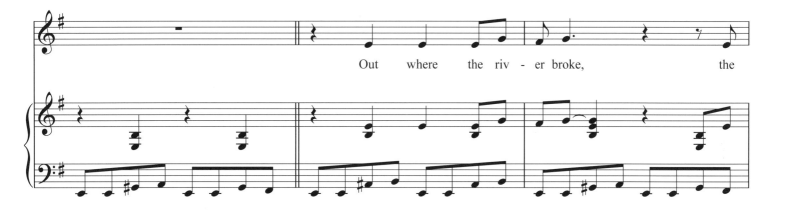

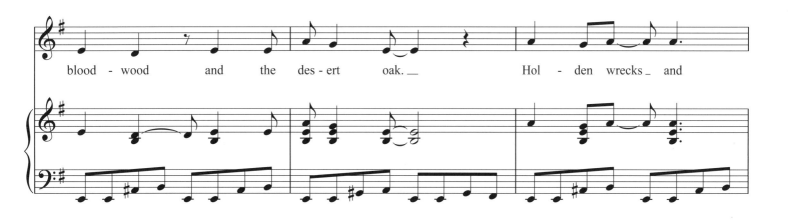

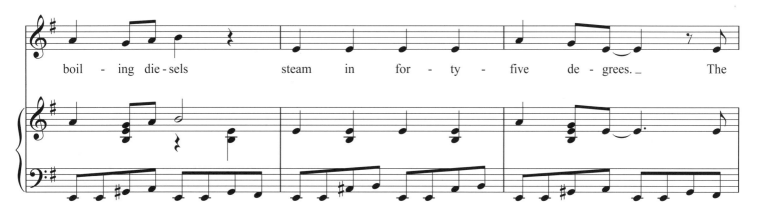

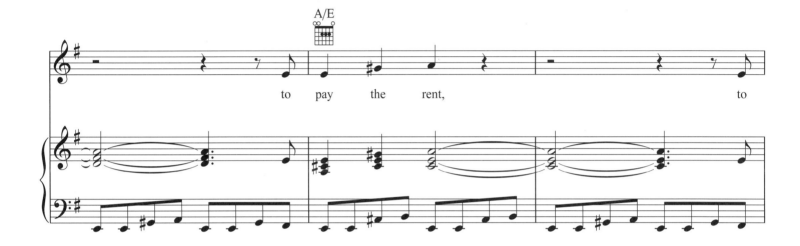

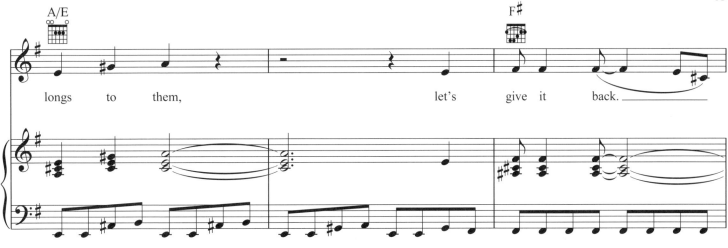

longs   to   them,   let's   give   it   back. _____

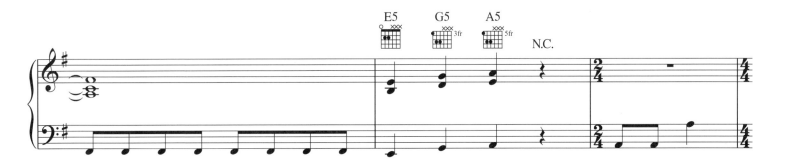

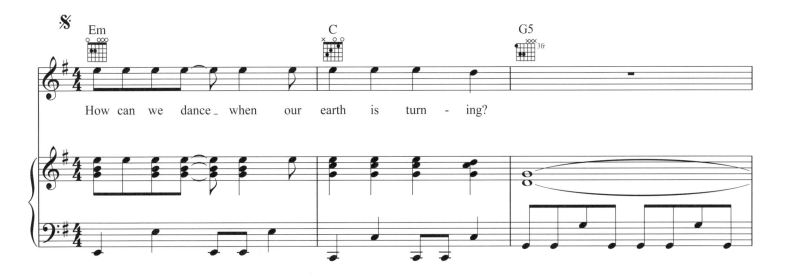

How can we dance _ when   our   earth   is   turn - ing?

How do we sleep _ while   our   beds   are   burn - ing?

How can we dance＿ when our

earth is turn - ing?

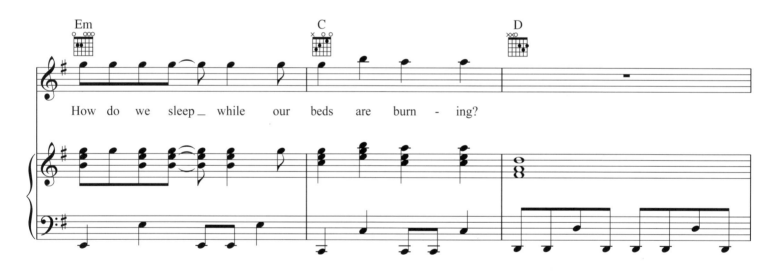

How do we sleep＿ while our beds are burn - ing?

The time has come to say fair's fair, to

pay our rent __ now, to pay our share. __

Four wheels scare the cock - a - toos _____ from

Kin - tore East to Yuen - de - mu. __ The west - ern des - ert

lives and breathes in for - ty - five de - grees. _____ The

time has come to say fair's fair,

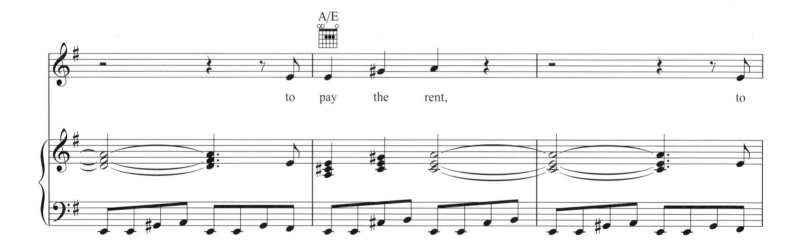

to pay the rent, to

pay our share. _ The time has come,

a fact's a fact. __ It be-

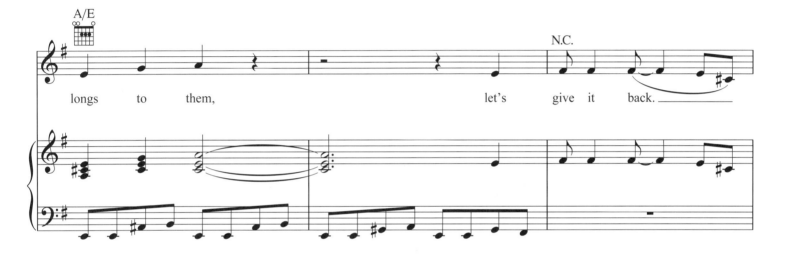

longs to them, let's give it back. _____

D.S. al Coda

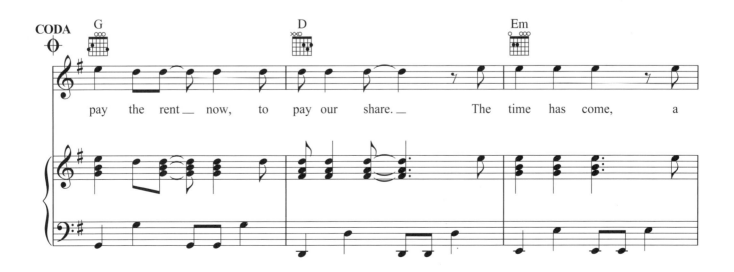

CODA

pay the rent __ now, to pay our share. __ The time has come, a

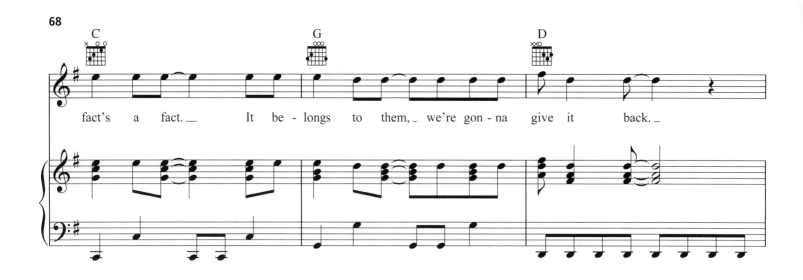

fact's a fact. _ It be- longs to them, _ we're gon- na give it back. _

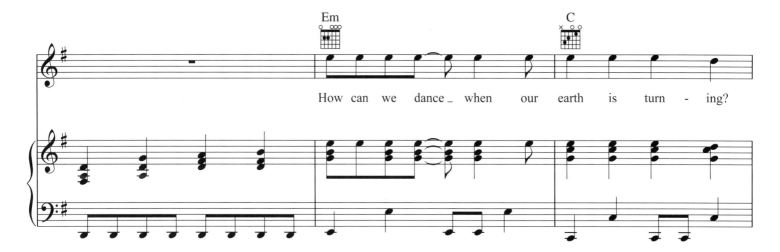

How can we dance _ when our earth is turn - ing?

How do we sleep _ while our

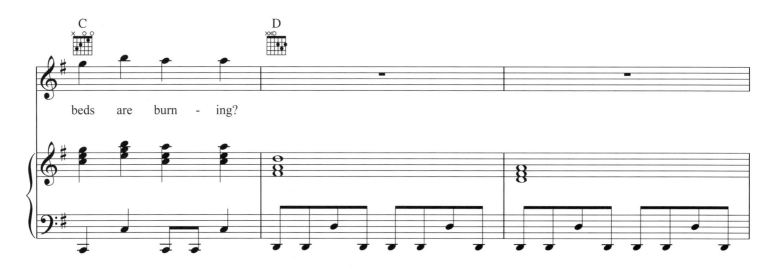

beds are burn - ing?

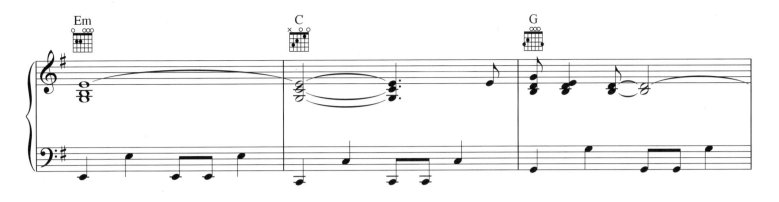

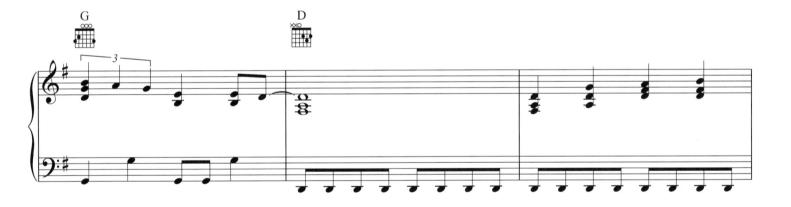

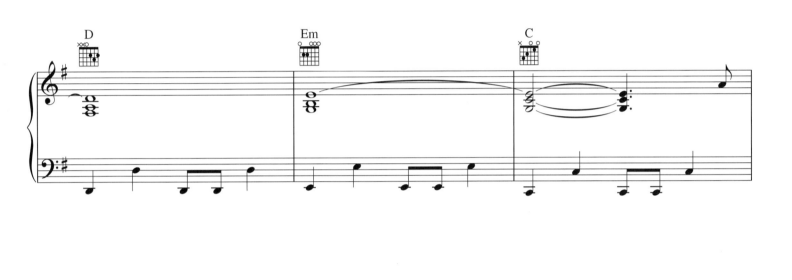

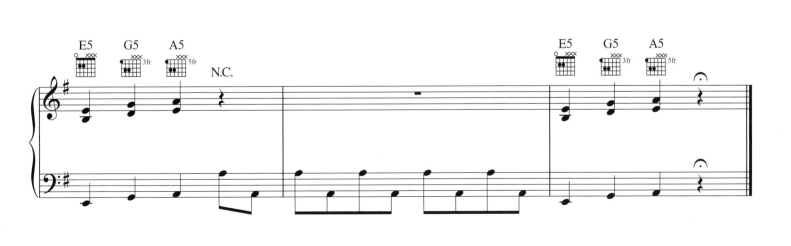

ONE COUNTRY

Words and Music by JAMES MOGINIE
and PETER GARRETT

Moderately, with intensity

Who'd like to change the world? _ Who wants to shoot the curl? _
Who hands out e - qual rights? _ Who starts and ends that fight? _
Who can make hard - won gains _ fall like the sum - mer rains? _

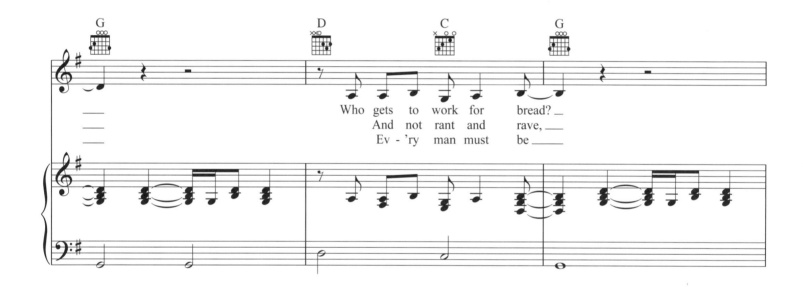

Who gets to work for bread? _
And not rant and rave, _
Ev - 'ry man must be _

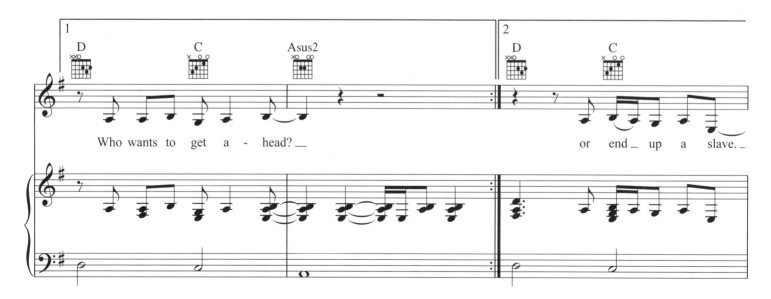

1

Who wants to get a - head? _

2

or end _ up a slave. _

what his life can be. ___ So

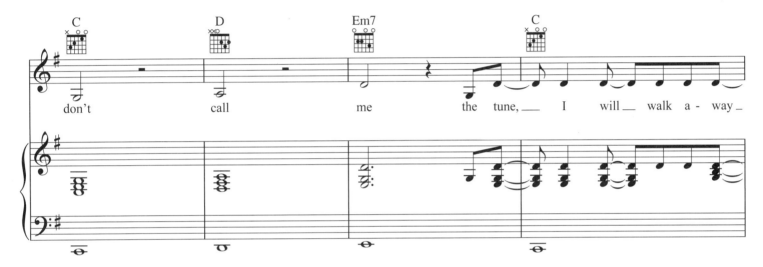

don't call me the tune, ___ I will ___ walk a - way ___

Who wants to please ev - 'ry - one? ___

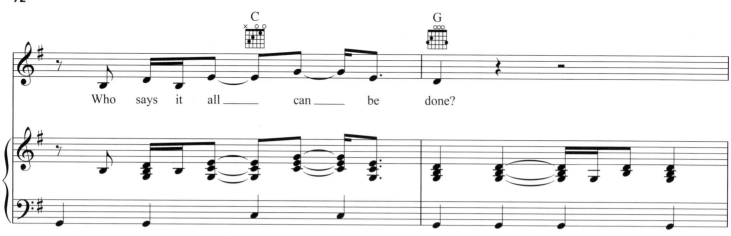

Who says it all _____ can _____ be done?

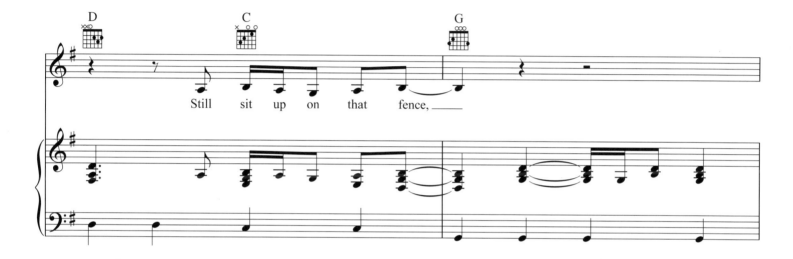

Still sit up on that fence, _____

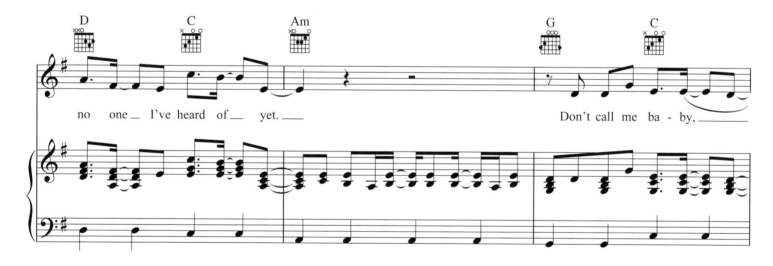

no one ___ I've heard of ___ yet. _____ Don't call me ba - by, _____

_____ don't talk in may - bes. _____

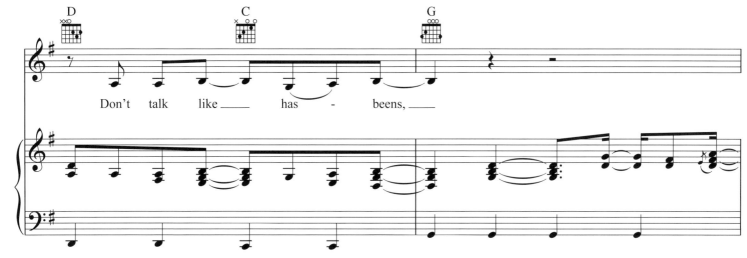

Don't talk like _____ has - beens, _____

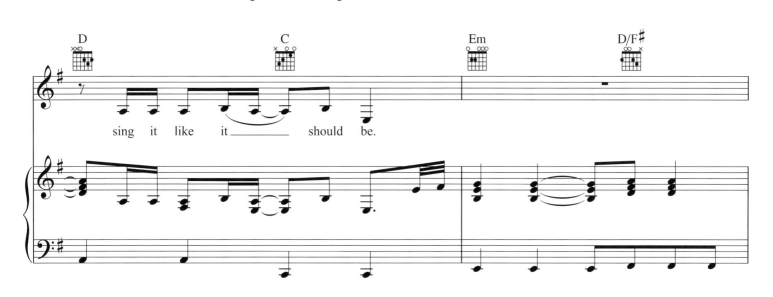

sing it like it _____ should be.

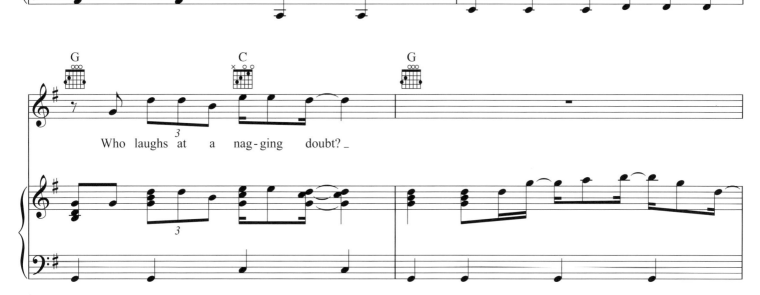

Who laughs at a nag-ging doubt? _

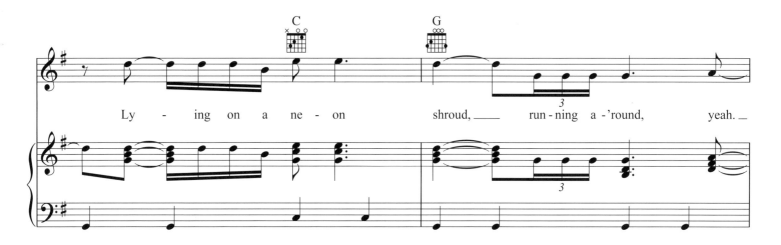

Ly - ing on a ne - on shroud, _____ run-ning a-'round, yeah. _

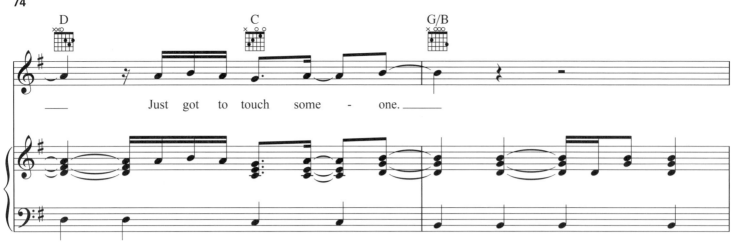

Just got to touch some - one. _____

Hey, __ I want to be. _____ So don't

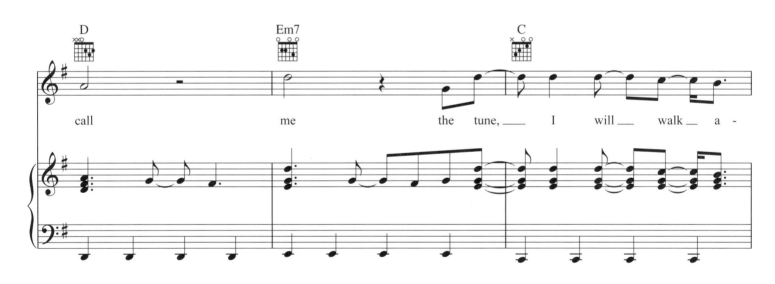

call me the tune, __ I will __ walk a -

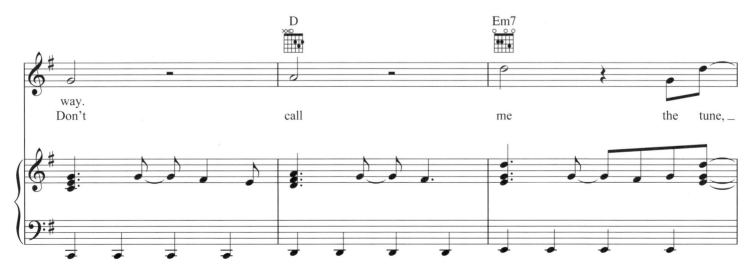

way. Don't call me the tune, __

I will __ walk __ a - way. Don't call

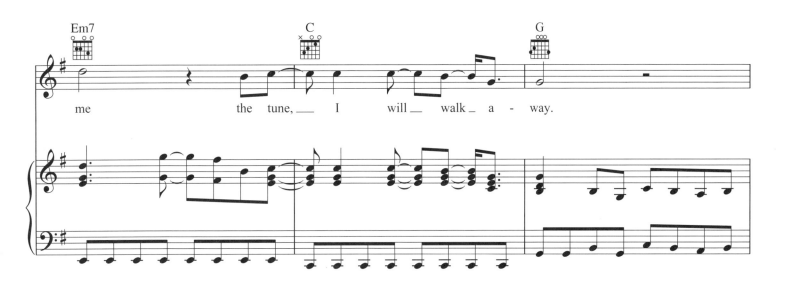

me the tune, __ I will __ walk __ a - way.

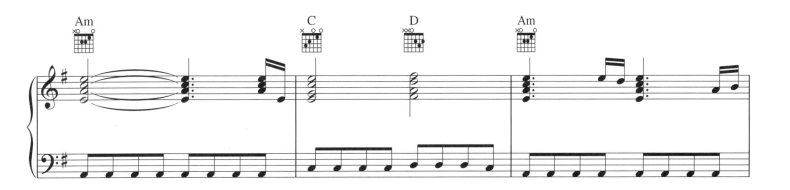

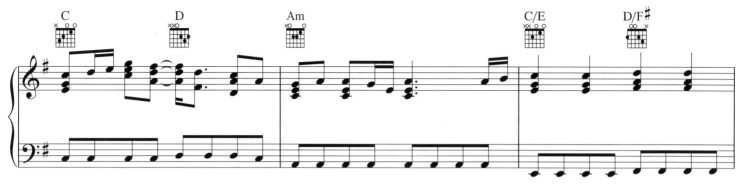

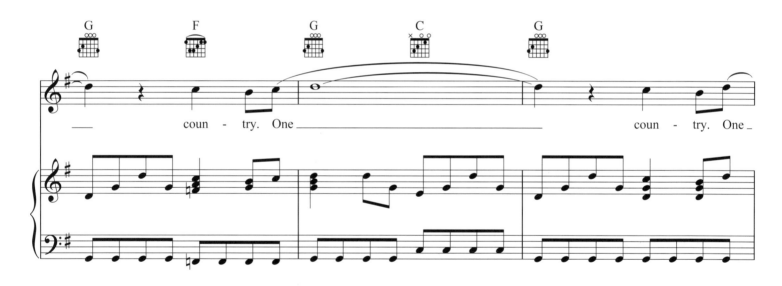

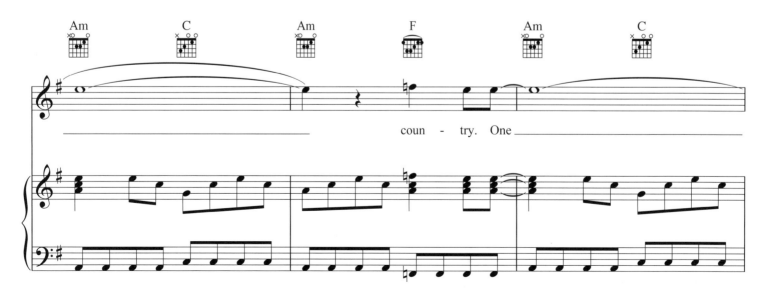

One vis - ion, one peo - ple, one land __ mass,

One __ country. One

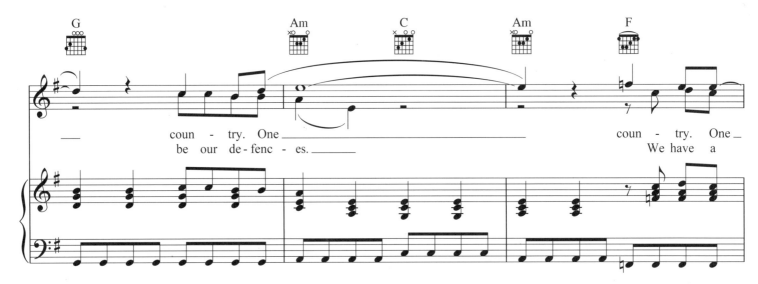

__ country. One

be our de - fenc - es. __

country. One __

We have a

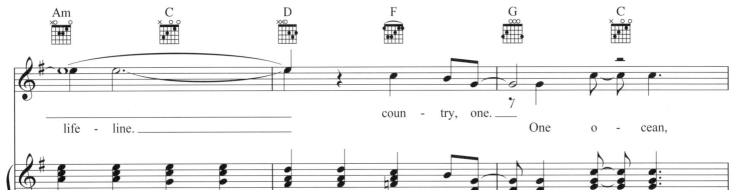

life - line. __

country, one. __

One o - cean,

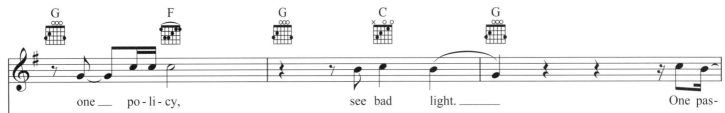

one __ po - li - cy,

see bad light. __

One pas-

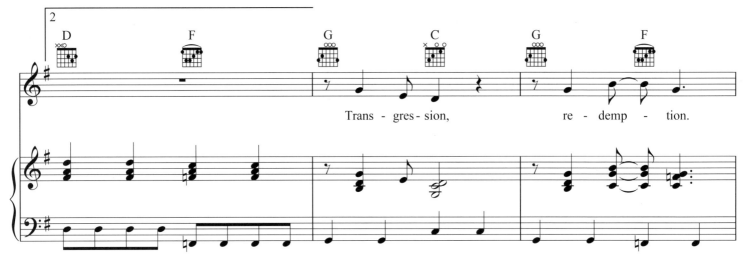

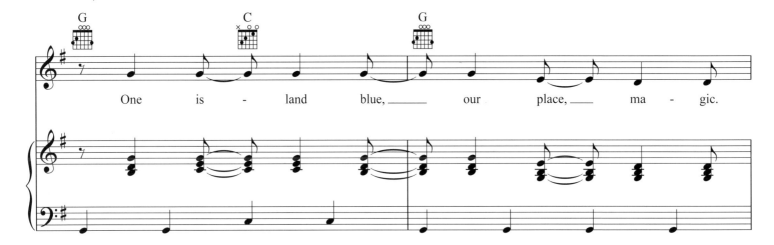

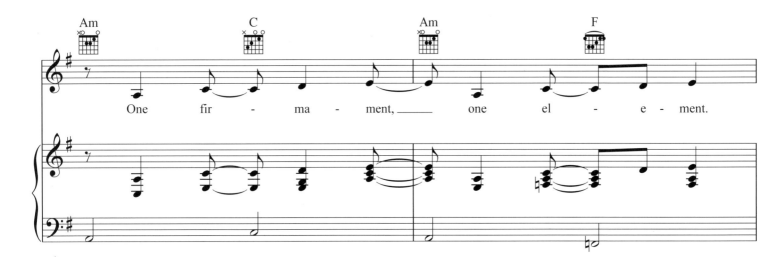

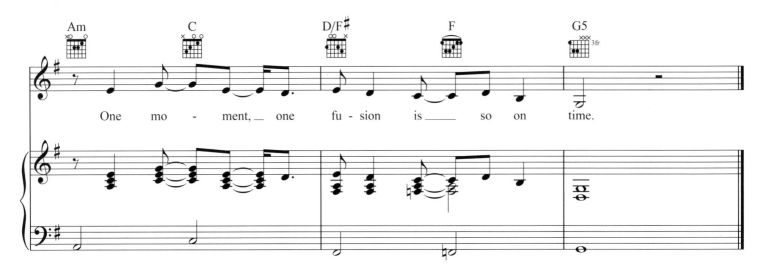

BEST OF BOTH WORLDS

Words and Music by ROBERT HIRST
and JAMES MOGINIE

Driving Rock beat

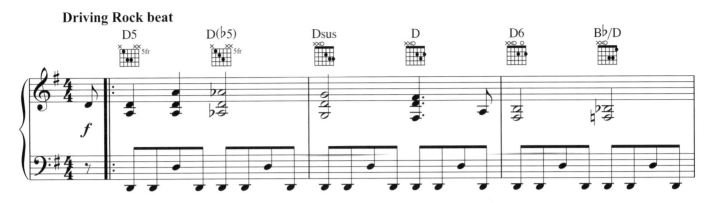

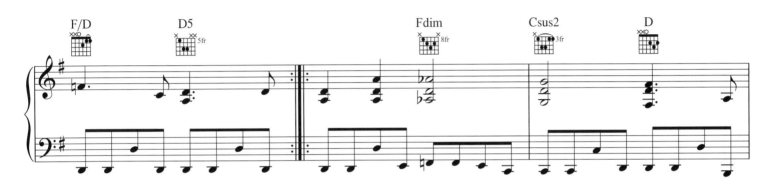

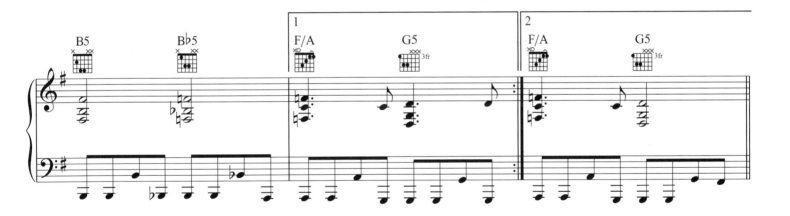

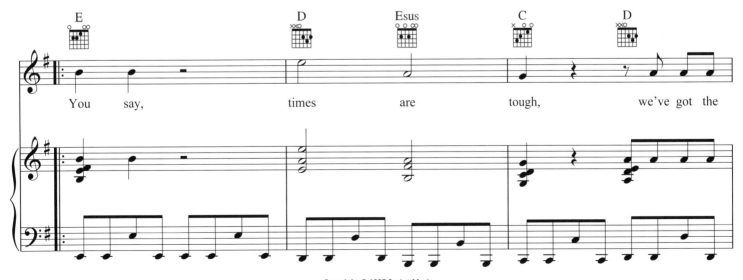

You say, times are tough, we've got the

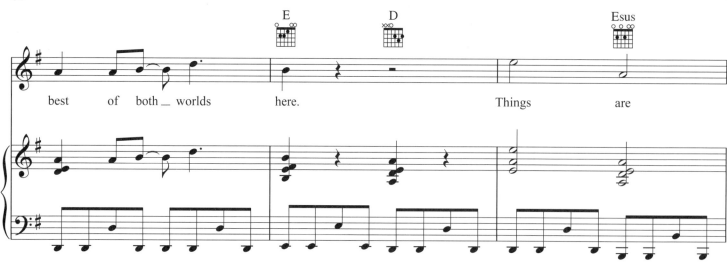

best of both __ worlds here. Things are

rough, we've got the best of both __ worlds here.

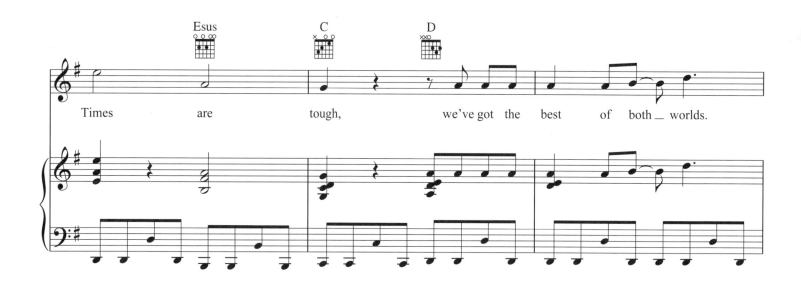

Times are tough, we've got the best of both __ worlds.

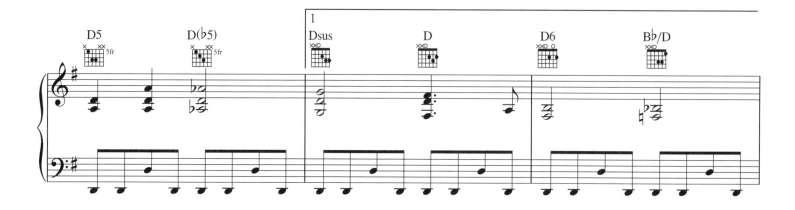

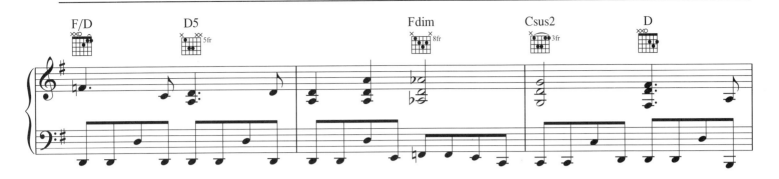

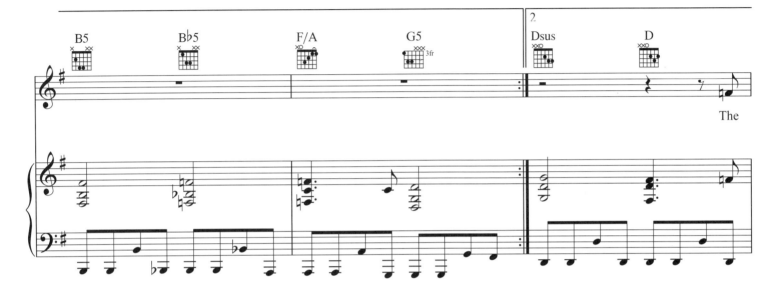

real world   is   not as   calm _ as it ap - pears   to be _ from   here. _
real world   is   not as   calm _ as it ap - pears   to be _ from   here. _

_ The real   world   is   not as   calm _ as it ap -
_ The small world   is   not as   strong _ and _ the

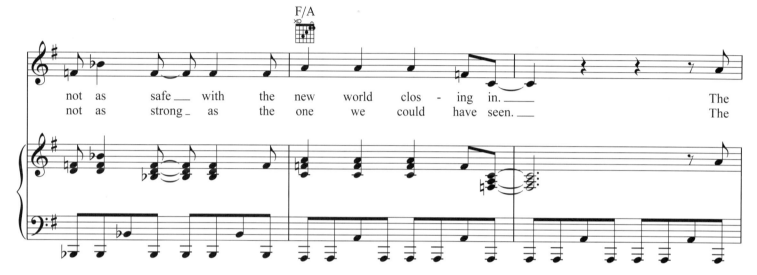

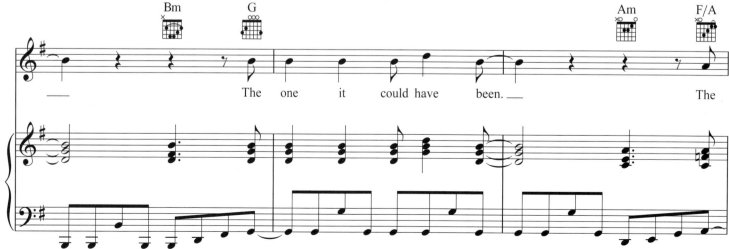

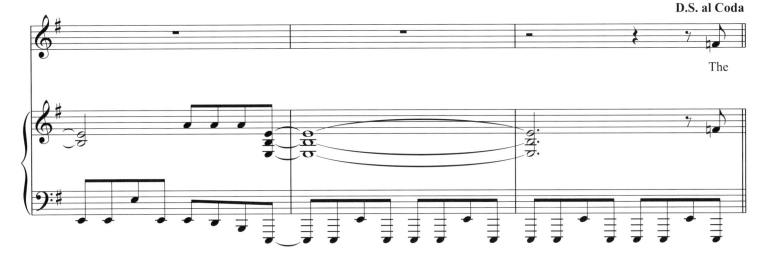

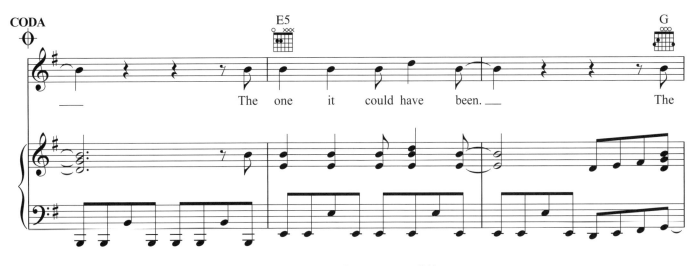

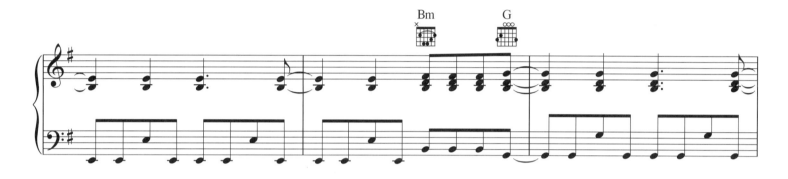

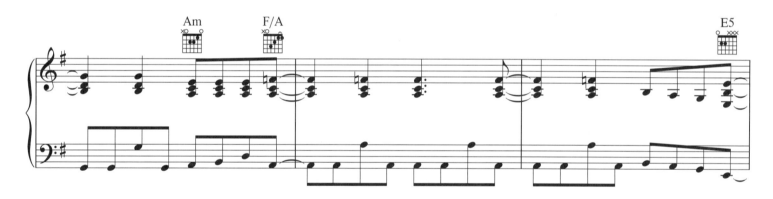

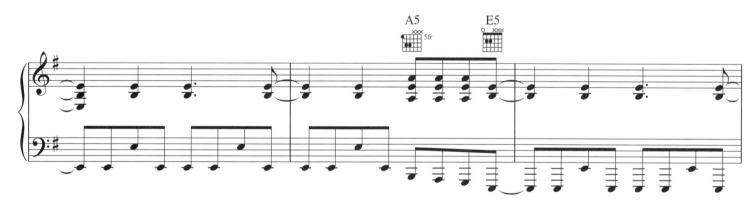

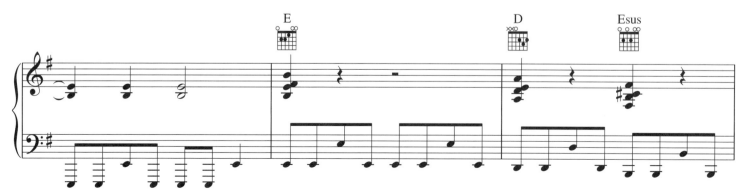

You say, you say,

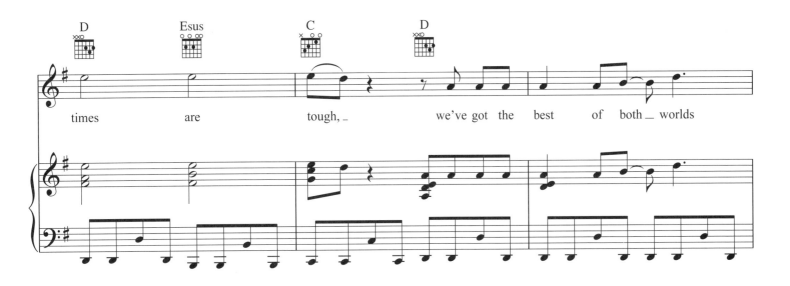

times are tough, we've got the best of both worlds

here. Things are rough, we've got the

TRUGANINI

Words and Music by ROBERT HIRST
and JAMES MOGINIE

Driving Rock beat

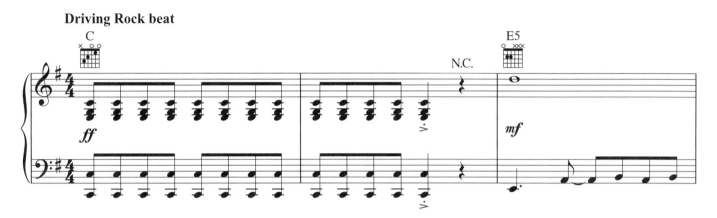

There's a road ___ train go-ing no-

We'll be stay-ing at the Ro-

where.
- ma bar

Roads are __
'til that

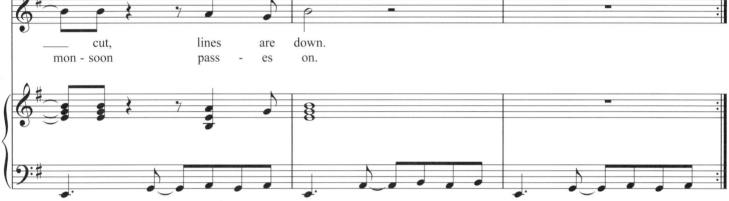

__ cut, lines are down.
mon - soon pass - es on.

E5

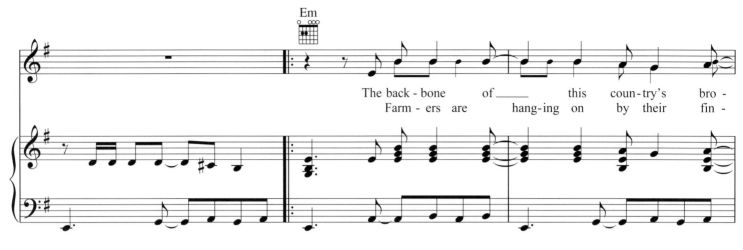

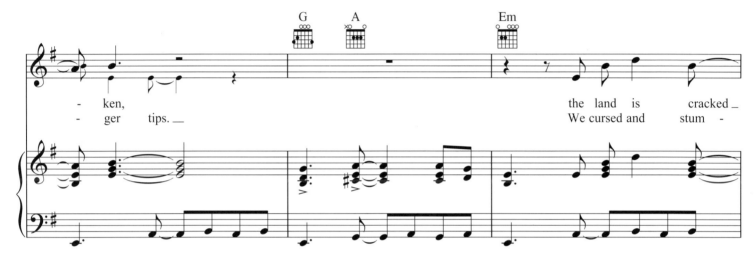

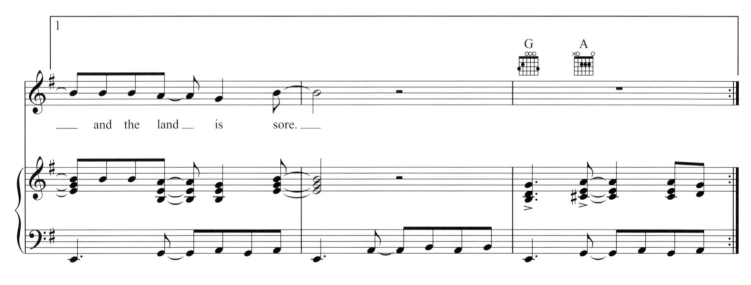

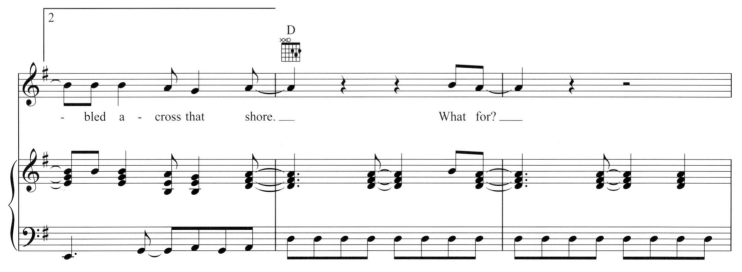

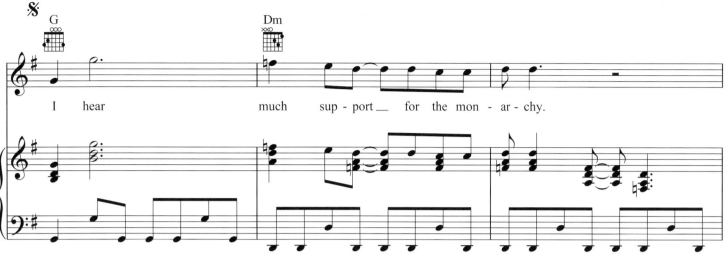

I hear much sup - port __ for the mon - ar - chy.

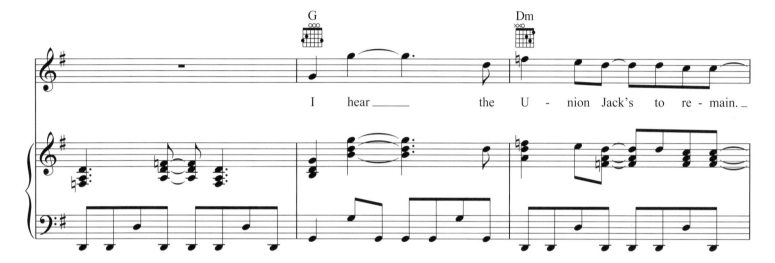

I hear _____ the U - nion Jack's to re - main. __

I see

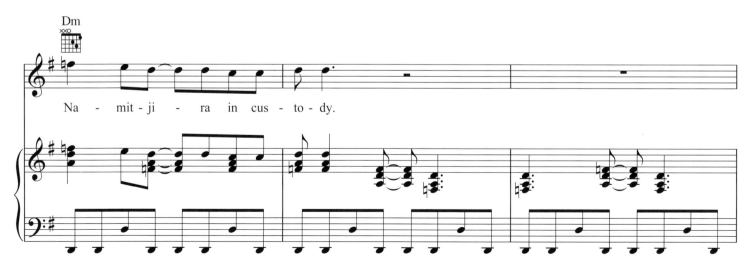

Na - mit - ji - ra in cus - to - dy.

To Coda

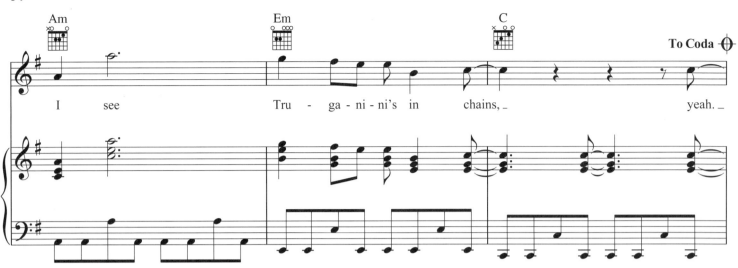

I see Tru - ga - ni - ni's in chains, _____ yeah. _____

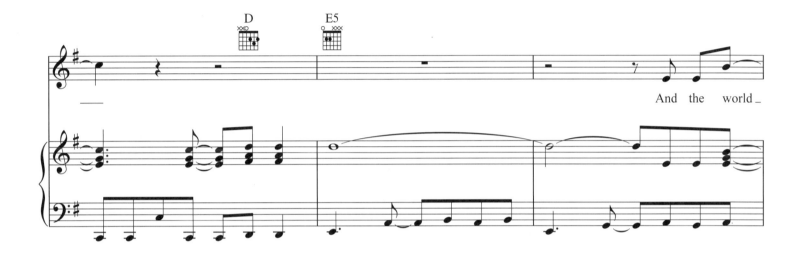

_____ And the world _____

_____ won't _ stand still. _____

And the world _____ won't _ stand still. _____

The blue col - lar work, __ it don't get you no - where.

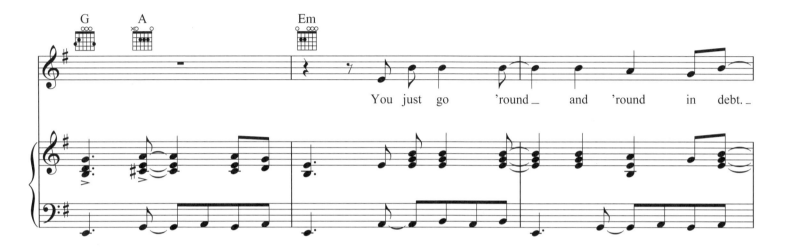

You just go 'round __ and 'round in debt. __

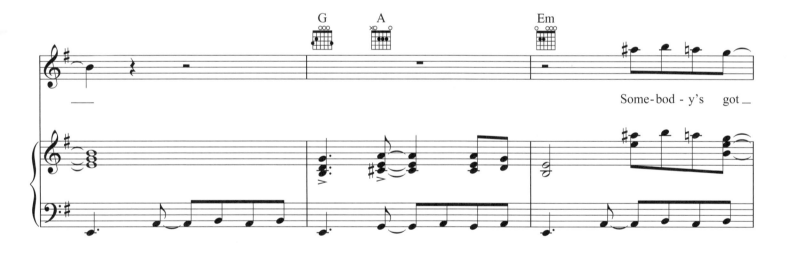

Some - bod - y's got __

__ you on __ that tread - mill, mate. __

And I hope you're ___ not beat-en yet, ___

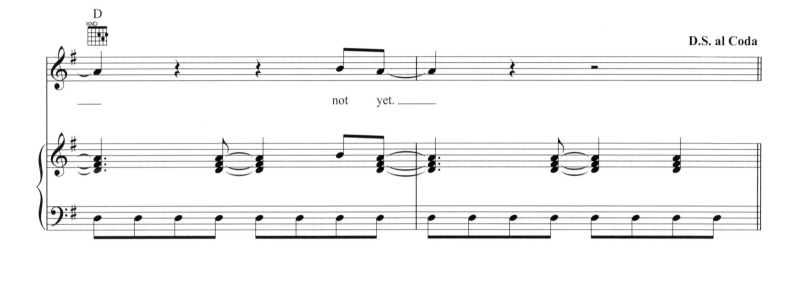

D.S. al Coda

___ not yet. ___

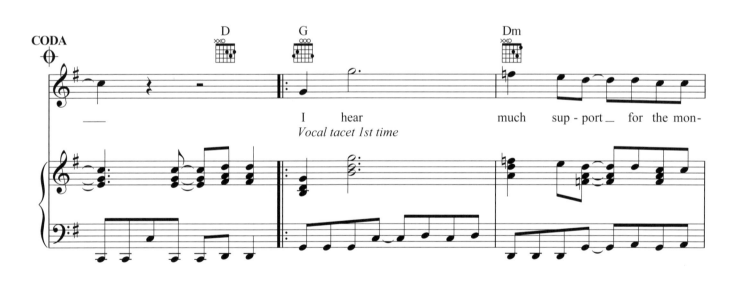

CODA

I hear much sup-port ___ for the mon-

Vocal tacet 1st time

ar - chy. I see ___ the

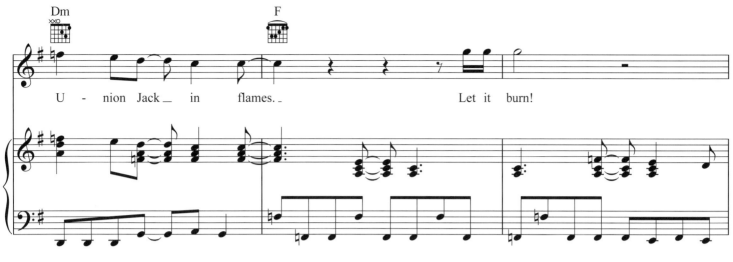

U - nion Jack __ in flames. __ Let it burn!

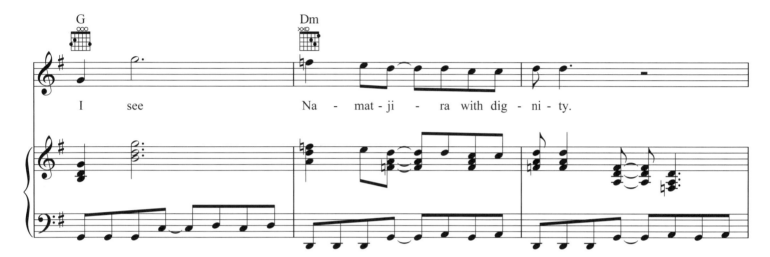

I see Na - mat - ji - ra with dig - ni - ty.

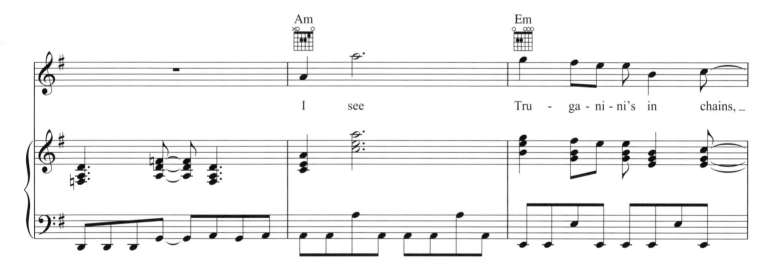

I see Tru - ga - ni - ni's in chains, __

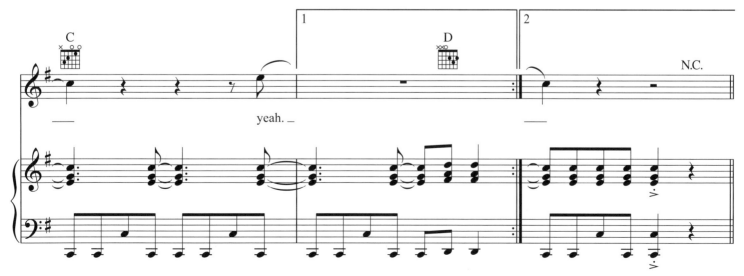

yeah. __

And the world __ won't __ stand still. __

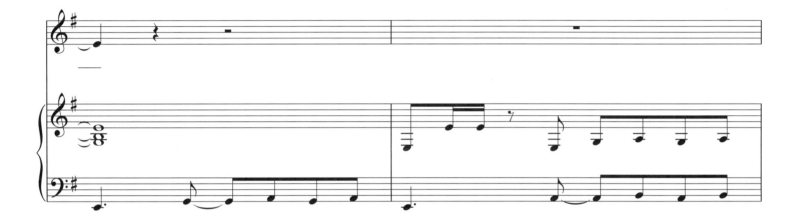

And the world _____ won't ___ stand still. __

BACK ON THE BORDERLINE

Words and Music by ANDREW JAMES,
PETER GARRETT and ROBERT HIRST

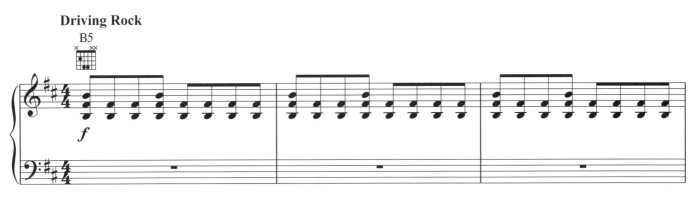

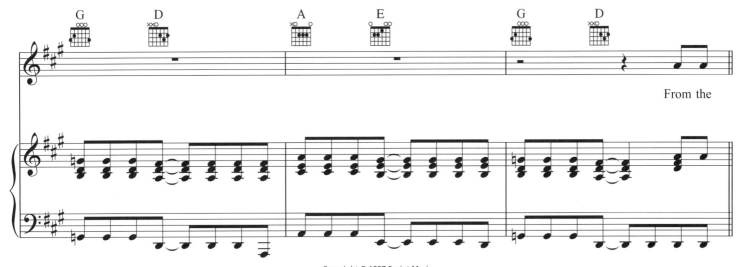

From the

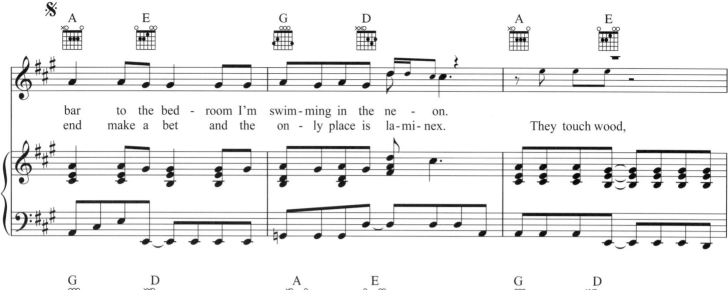

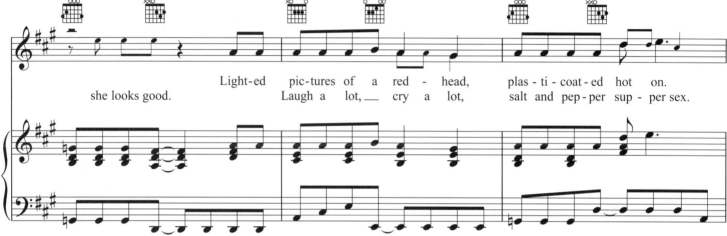

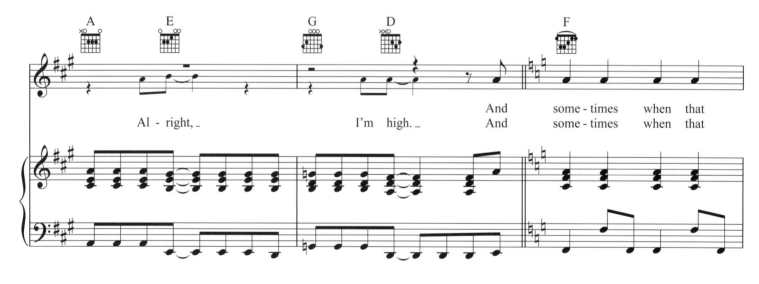

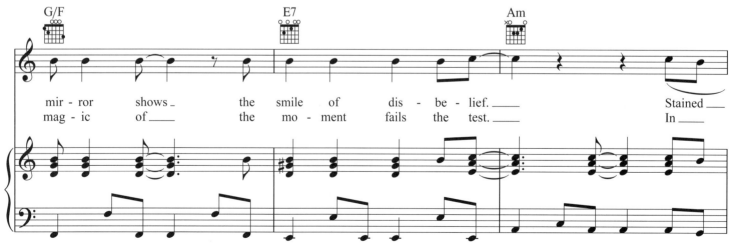

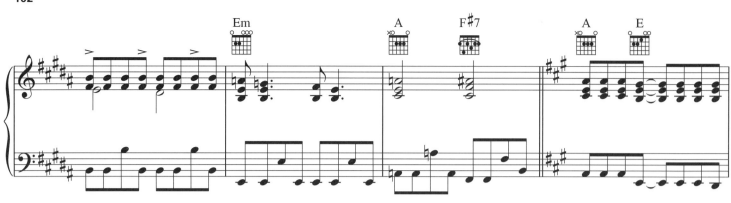

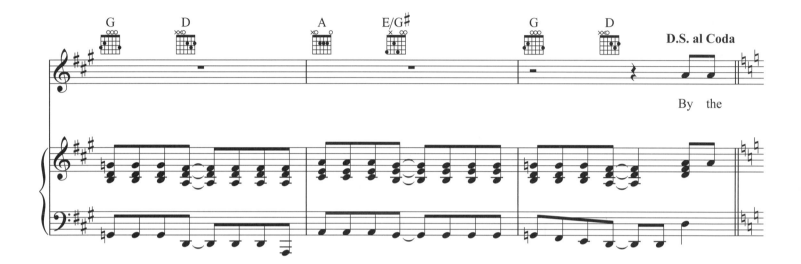

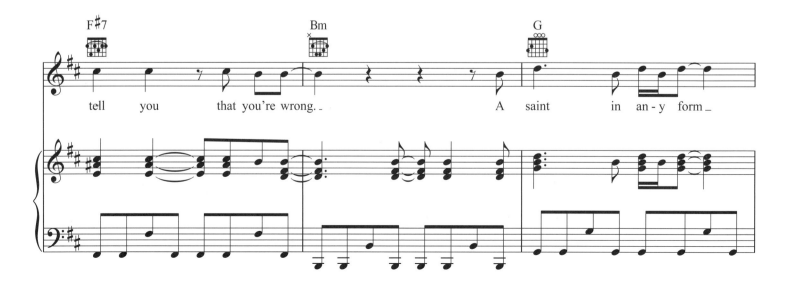

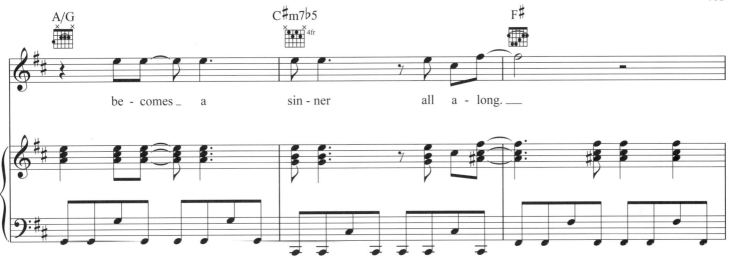

be - comes _ a sin - ner all a - long. __

I'm back on the bor - der - line.

Yes, I'm back on the bor - der - line.

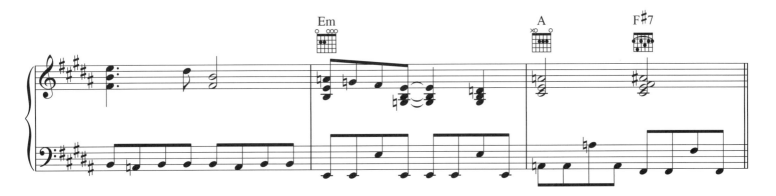

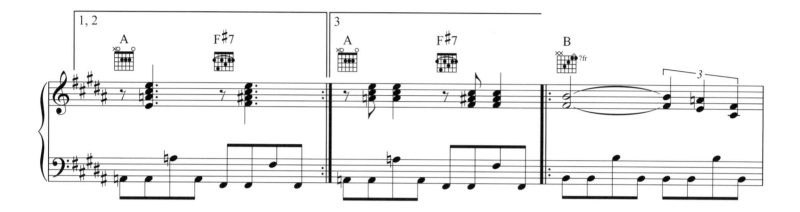

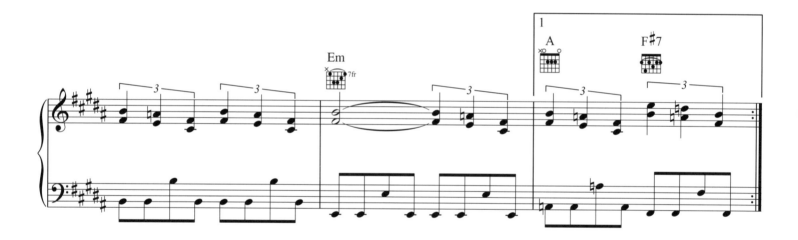

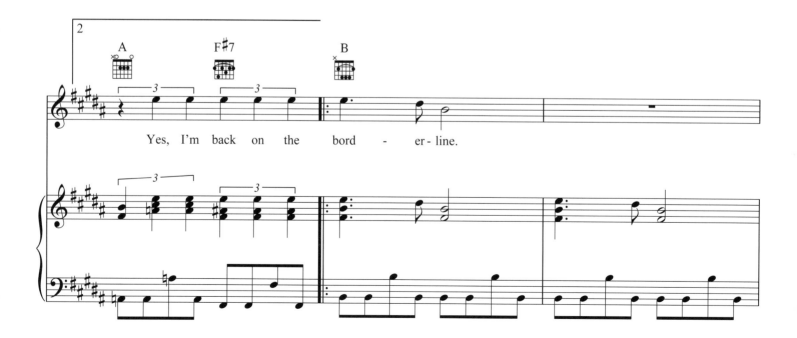

Yes, I'm back on the bord - er - line.

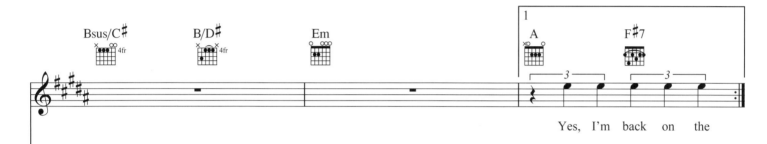

Yes, I'm back on the bor - der - line.

Yes, I'm back on the

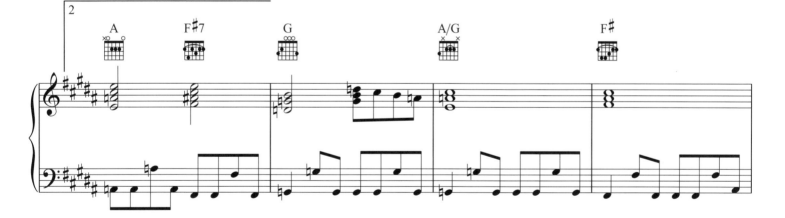

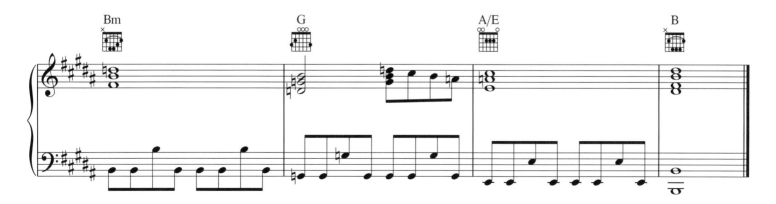

KING OF THE MOUNTAIN

Words and Music by ROBERT HIRST
and JAMES MOGINIE

With energy

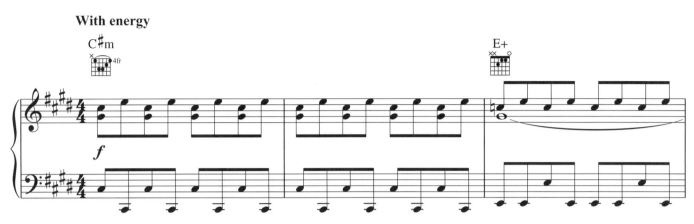

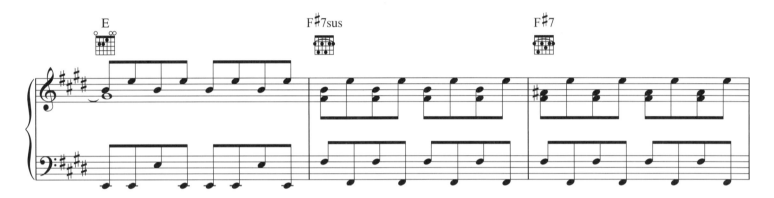

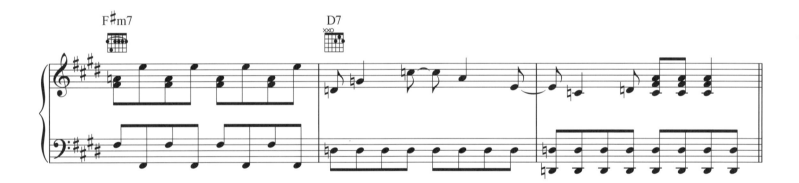

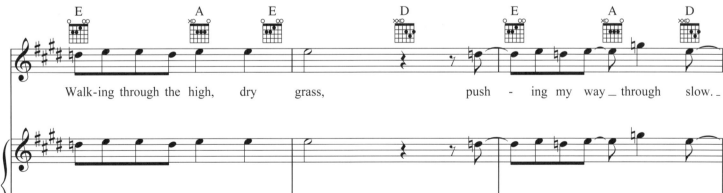

Walk-ing through the high, dry grass, push - ing my way __ through slow. __

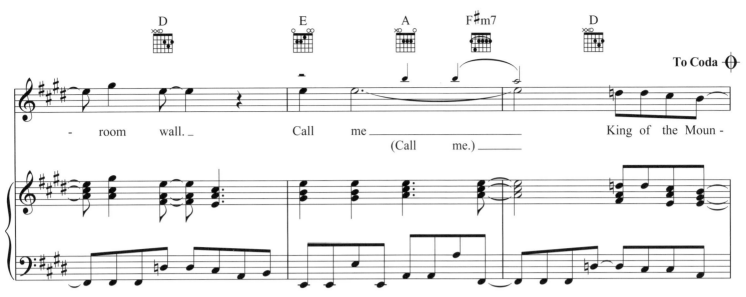

room wall. Call me King of the Moun-
(Call me.)

To Coda ⊕

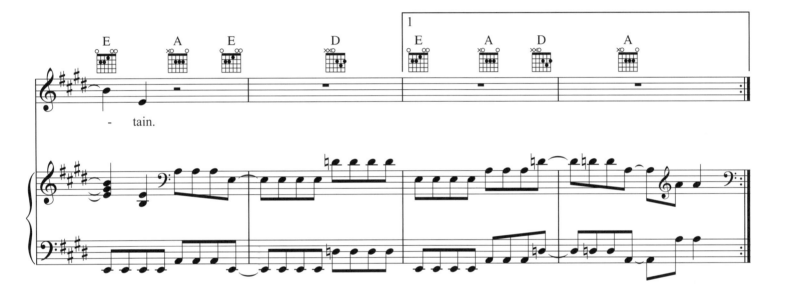

- tain.

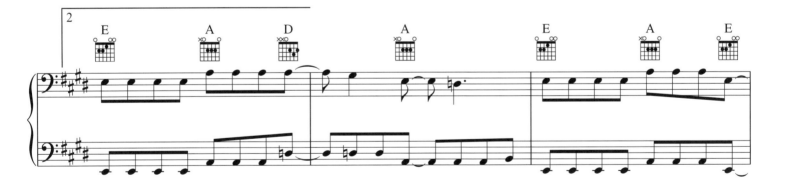

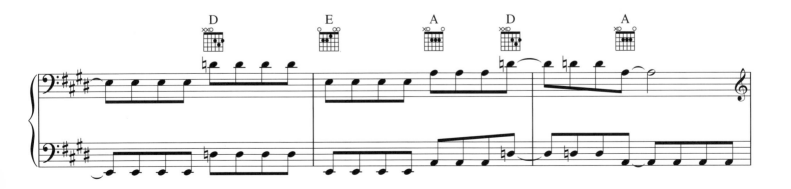

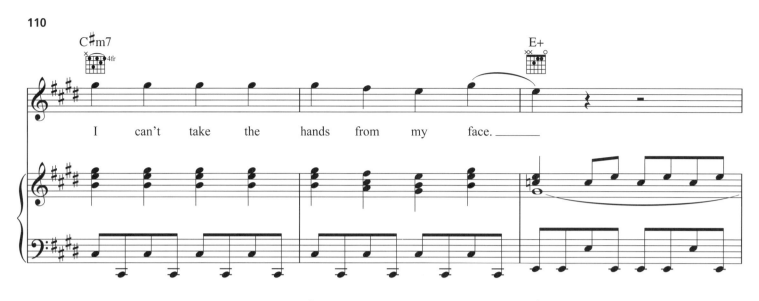

I can't take the hands from my face.

There are some things we can't re - place.

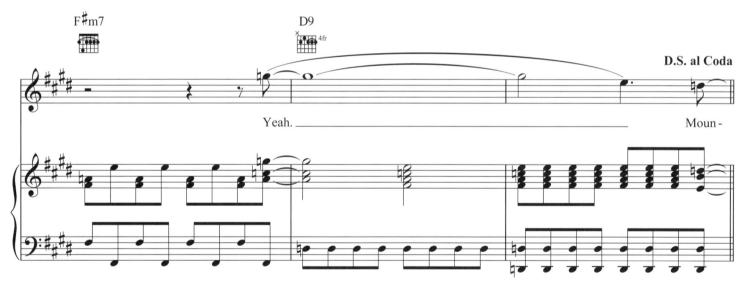

D.S. al Coda

Yeah. _____ Moun -

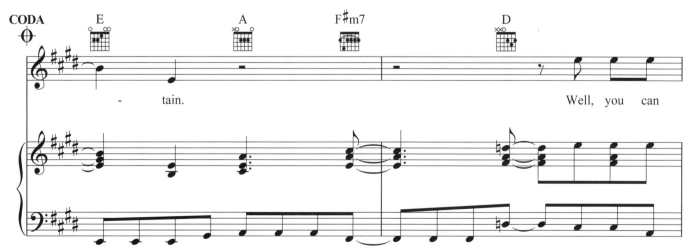

CODA

- tain. Well, you can

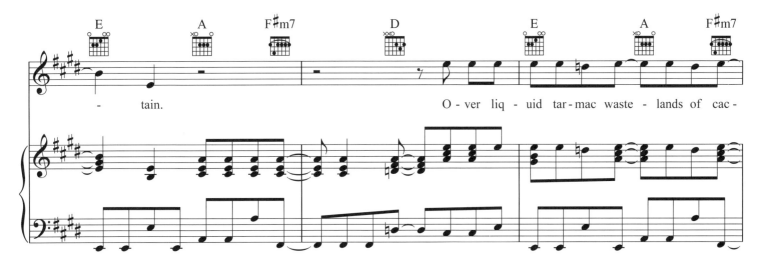

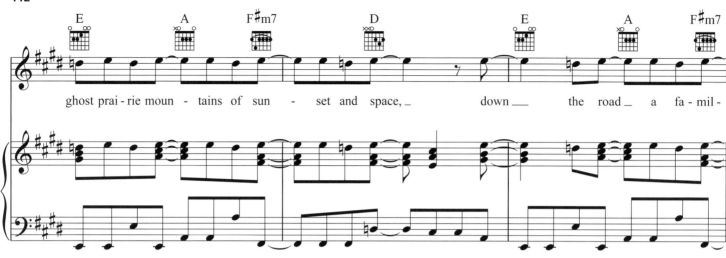

ghost prai - rie moun - tains of sun - set and space, ___ down ___ the road ___ a fa - mil -

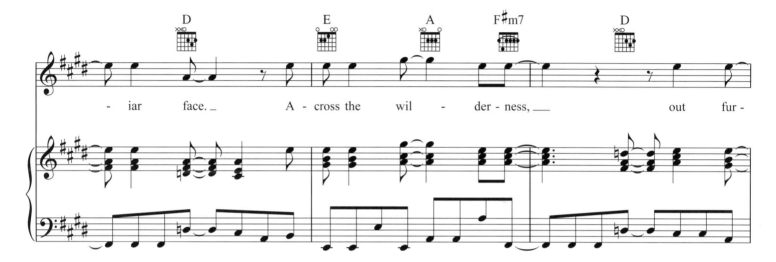

- iar face. ___ A - cross the wil - der - ness, ___ out fur -

- ther than ___ the bush, ___ I will fol - low you. ___

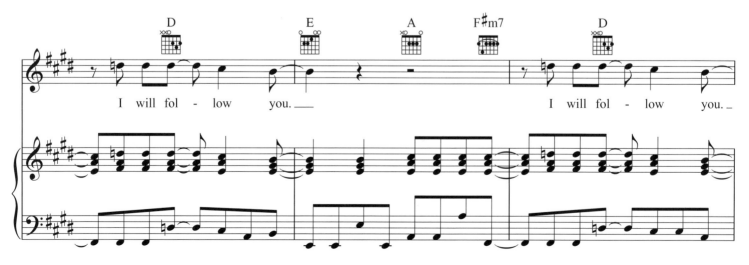

I will fol - low you. ___ I will fol - low you. __

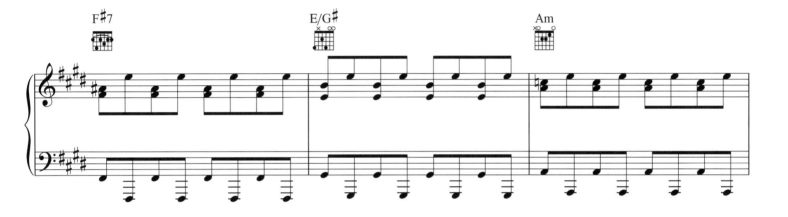

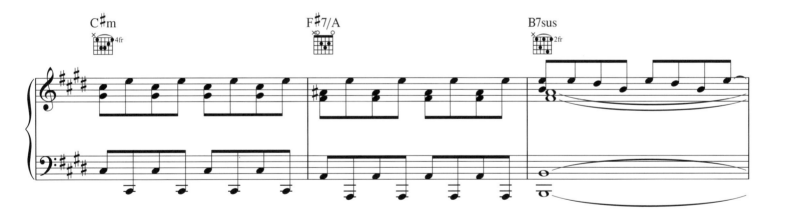

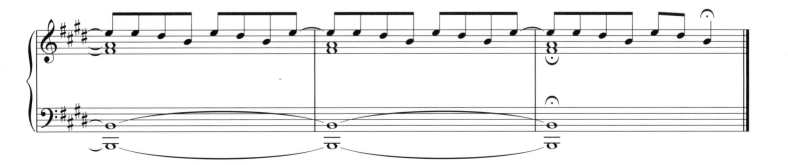

HERCULES

Words and Music by JAMES MOGINIE,
PETER GARRETT and ROBERT HIRST

Driving Rock

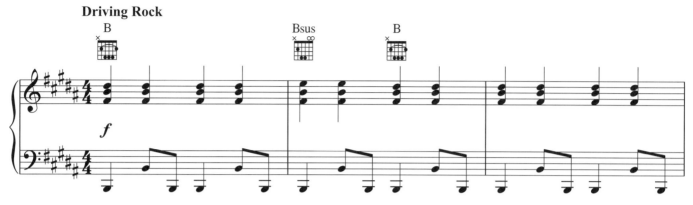

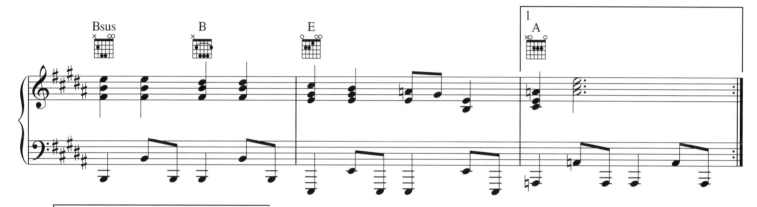

My life is a val-ua-ble thing,

I want to keep ___ it that way. I won't

cry.   My   life's   such   a   val-ua-ble   thing, _

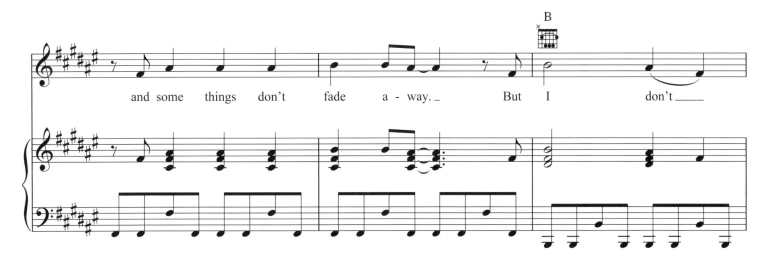

and   some   things   don't   fade   a-way. _   But   I   don't _____

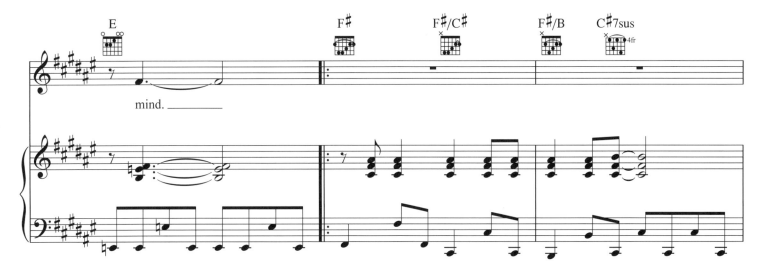

mind. _____

We   give   the   best _
It   seems   to   me   that   what _

116

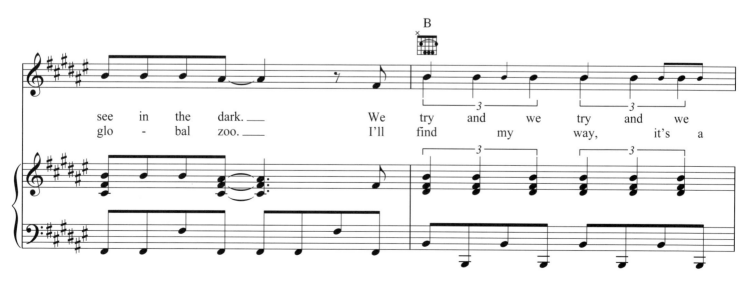

Here comes the Her - cu - les, ___ here comes the

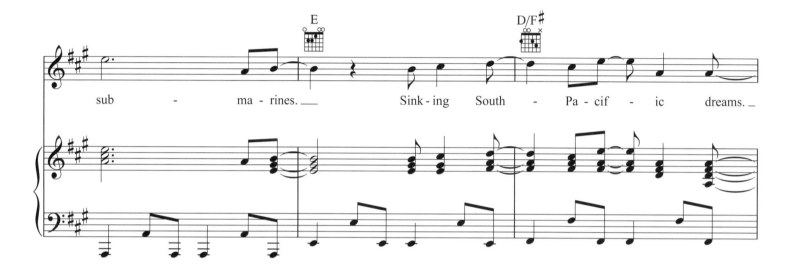

sub - ma - rines. ___ Sink - ing South - Pa - cif - ic dreams. ___

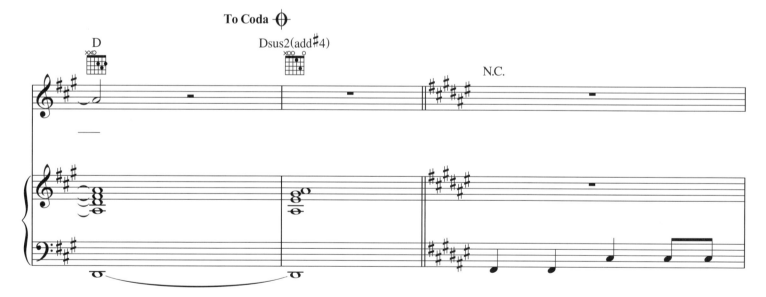

To Coda ⊕

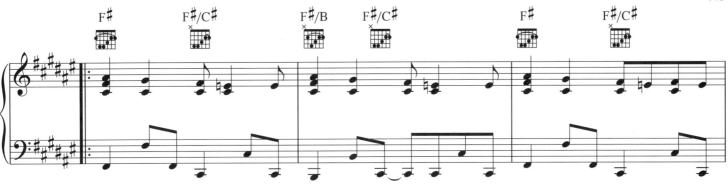

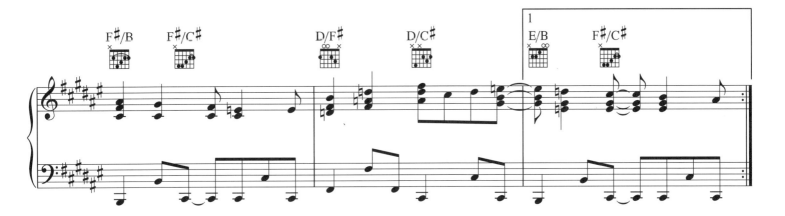

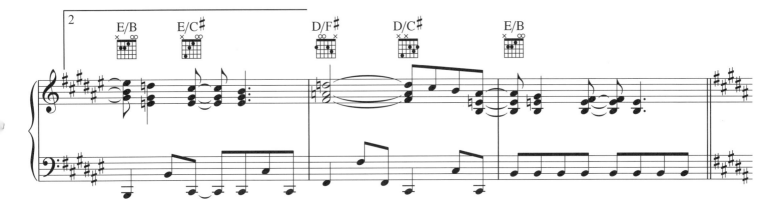

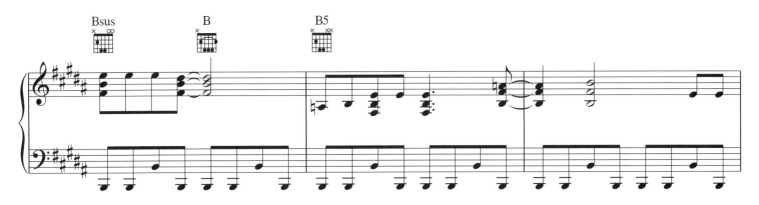

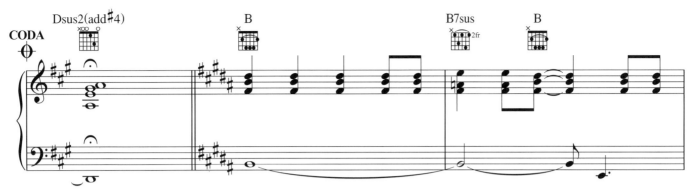

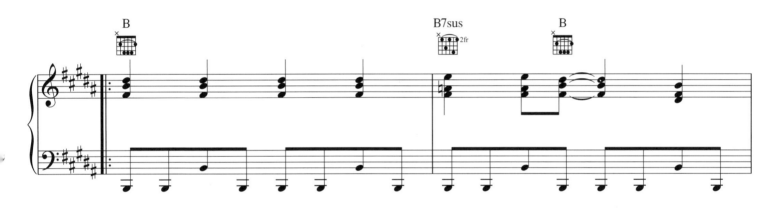

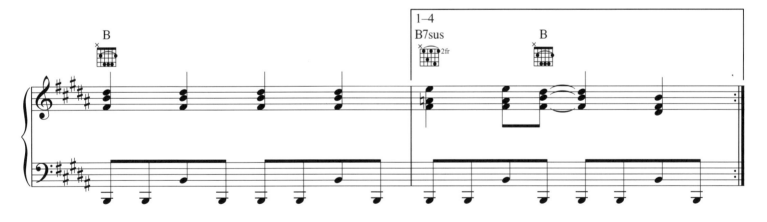

SURF'S UP TONIGHT

Words and Music by JAMES MOGINIE
and PETER GARRETT

Steady Rock beat

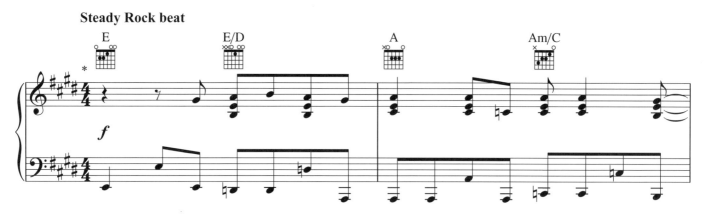

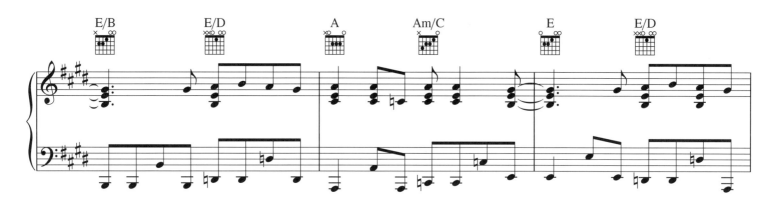

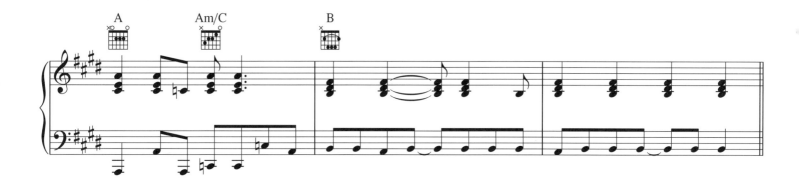

Wher - ev - er the wind___ blows____
Sum - mer's___ on___ hold,

* Recorded a half step lower.

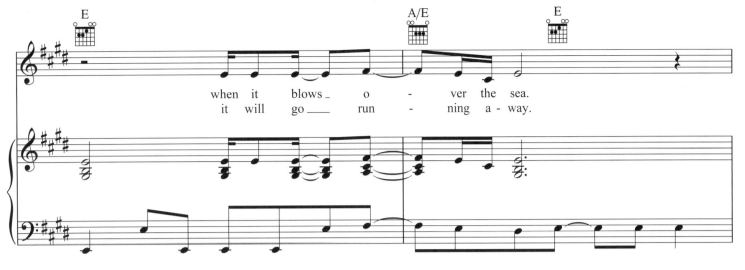

when it blows _ o - ver the sea.
it will go _ run - ning a - way.

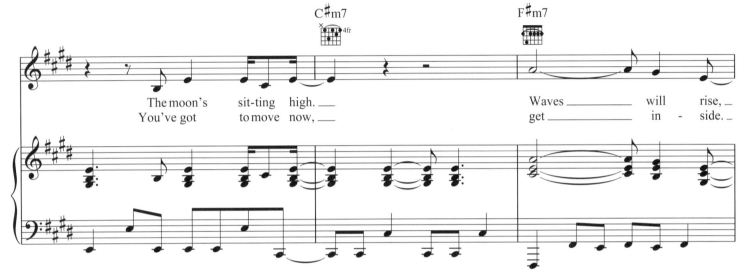

The moon's sit-ting high. _
You've got to move now, _

Waves _ will rise, _
get _ in - side. _

_ wa - ter shapes, _
_ Take that dive. _

waves will take you take you there.
Get in - side _ to - day.

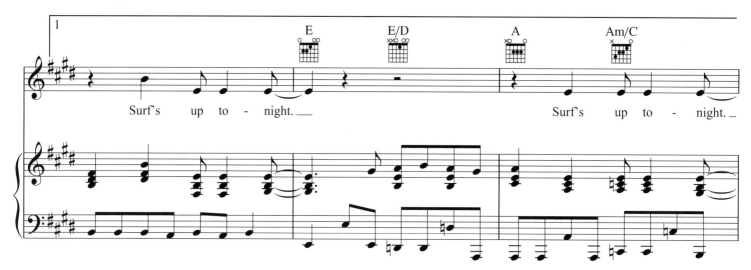

Surf's up to-night. ___ Surf's up to-night. ___

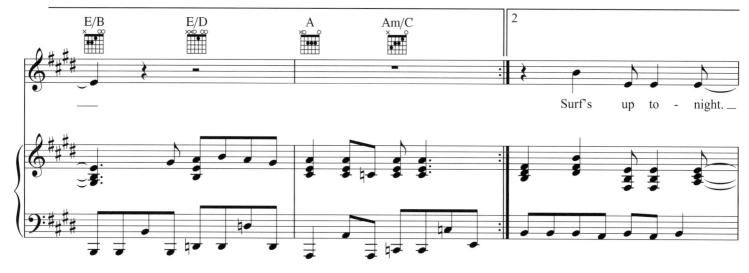

___ Surf's up to-night. ___

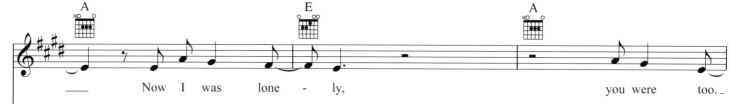

___ Now I was lone - ly, you were too. ___

___ I met you down ___ at the wa - ter - line. Now, ___

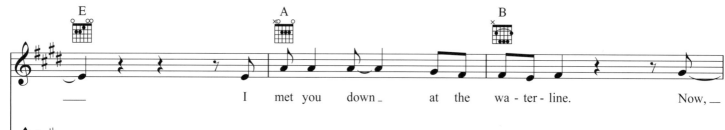

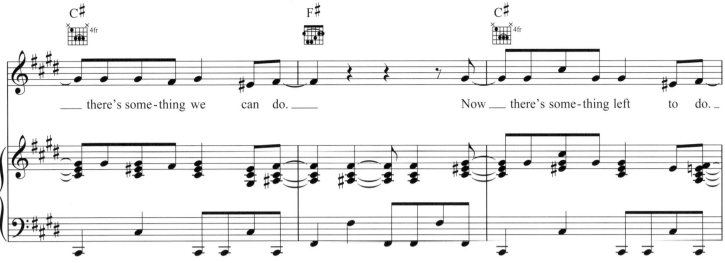

there's some-thing we can do. ___ Now ___ there's some-thing left to do. ___

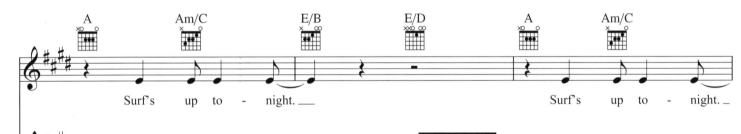

___ Oh, yeah.

Surf's up to - night. ___ Surf's up to - night. ___

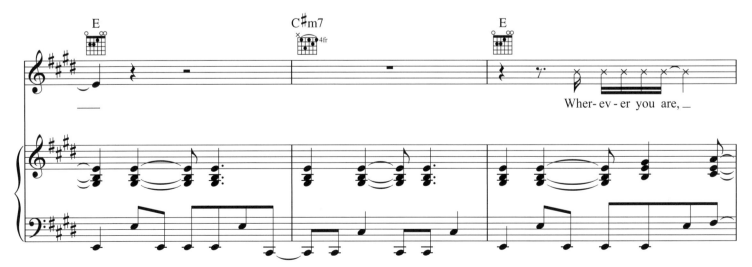

___ Wher- ev - er you are, ___

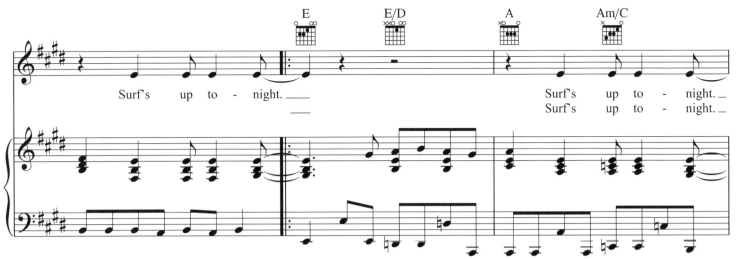

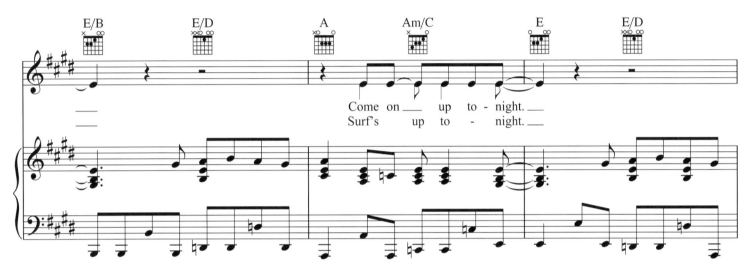

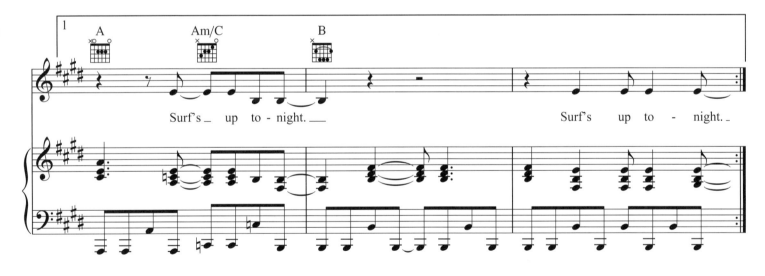

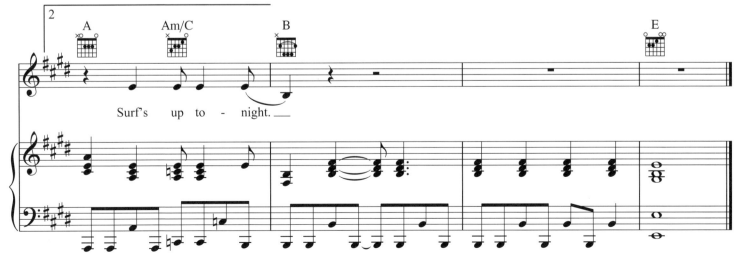

DON'T WANNA BE THE ONE

Words and Music by ROBERT HIRST,
PETER GARRETT, MARTIN ROTSEY
and JAMES MOGINIE

Driving Rock

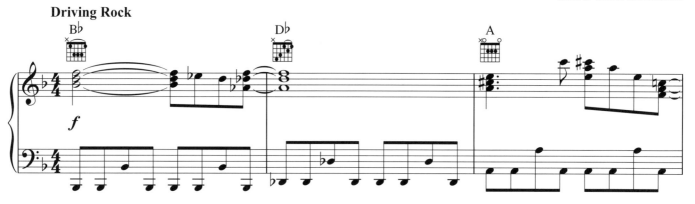

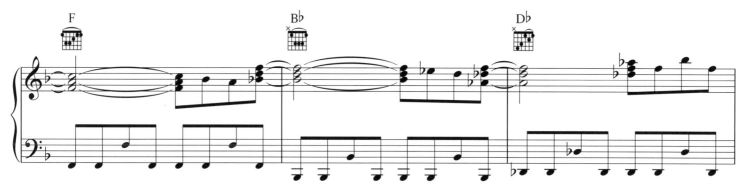

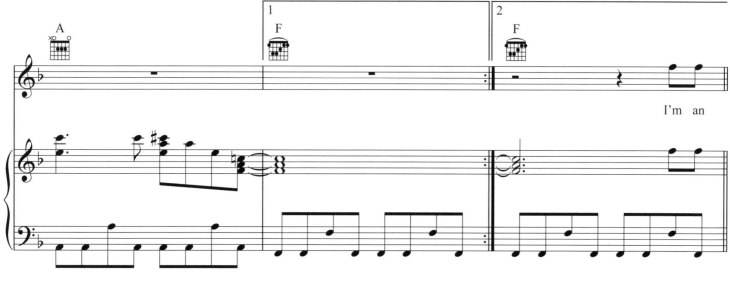

I'm an in-no-cent vic-tim, I'm just like you. We end up in home u-nits with a

brick wall __ view. I can't be - lieve the per - fect fam-'lies on my co - lour T - V. If I don't

make it to the top, it will nev - er both - er me. And I don't wan - na be the one.

And I don't wan - na be the one. And I don't

To Coda ⊕

wan - na be the one. And I don't wan - na be the one.

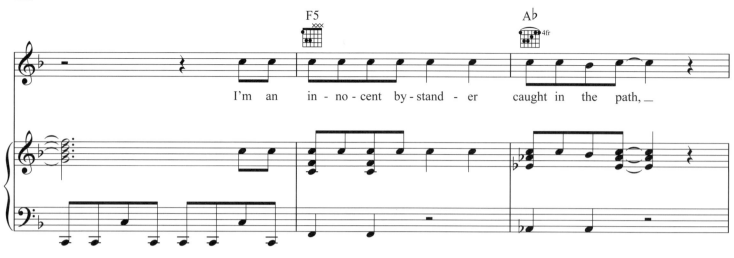

I'm an in-no-cent by-stand-er caught in the path,—

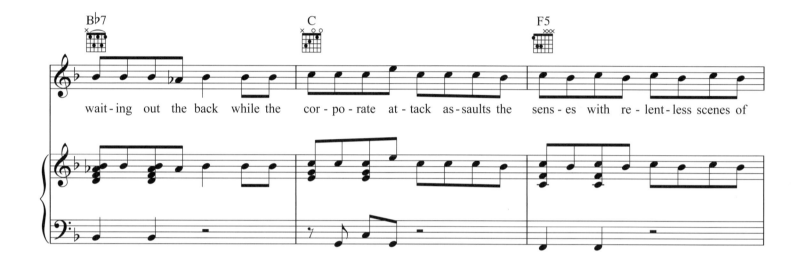

wait-ing out the back while the cor-po-rate at-tack as-saults the sens-es with re-lent-less scenes of

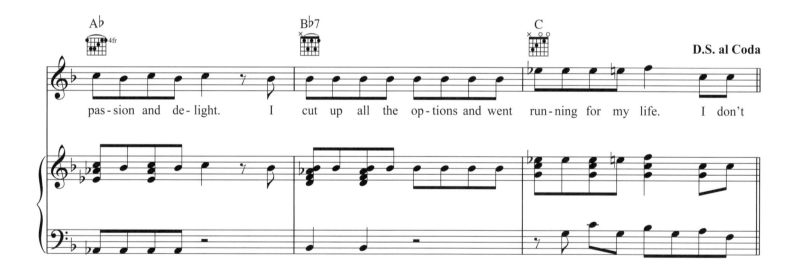

D.S. al Coda

pas-sion and de-light. I cut up all the op-tions and went run-ning for my life. I don't

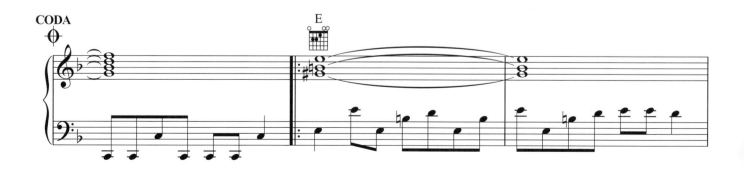

CODA

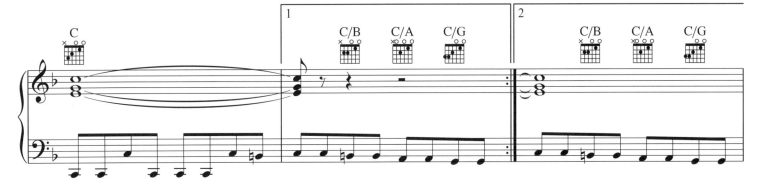

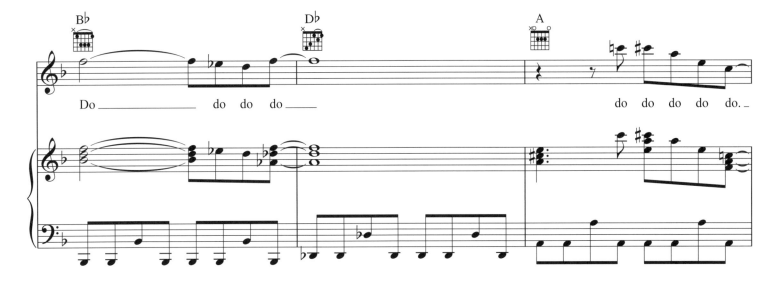

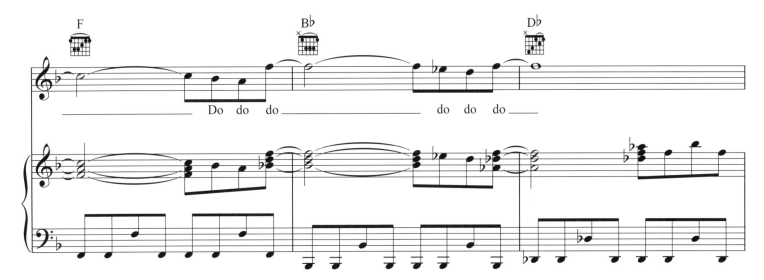

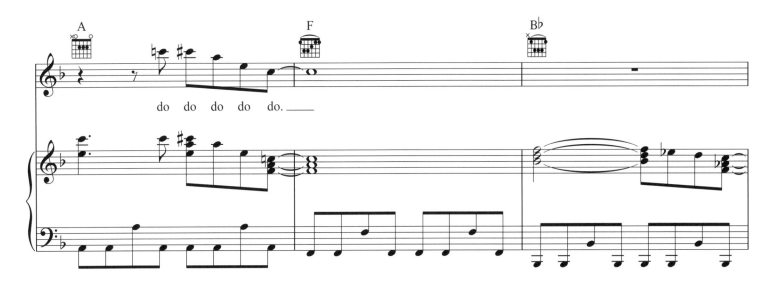

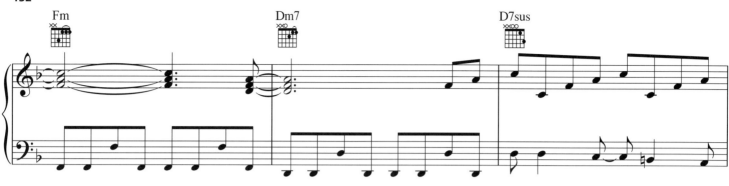

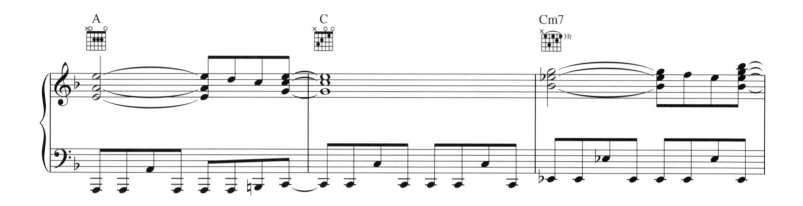

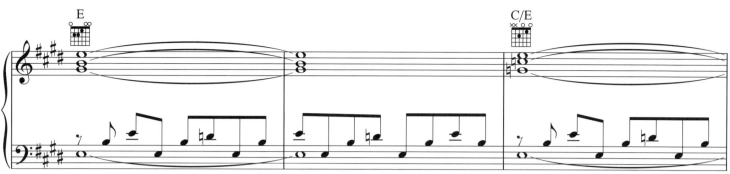

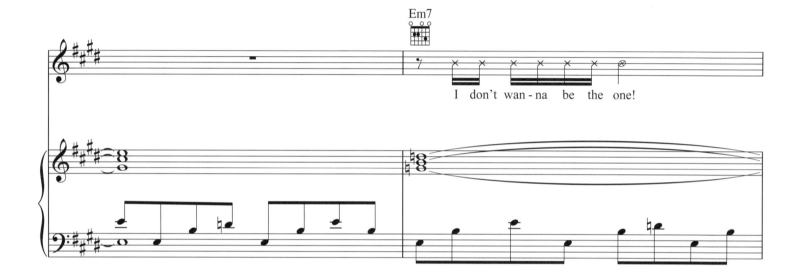

I don't wan-na be the one!

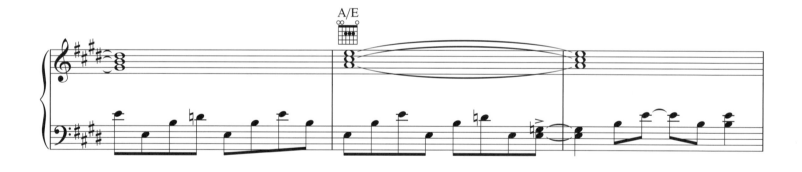

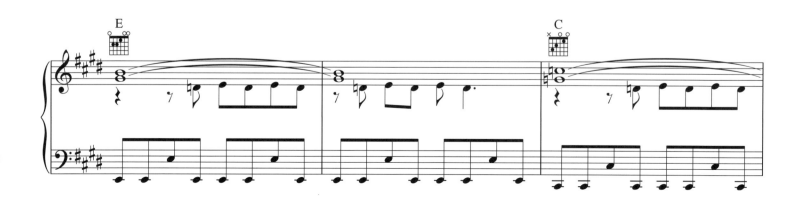

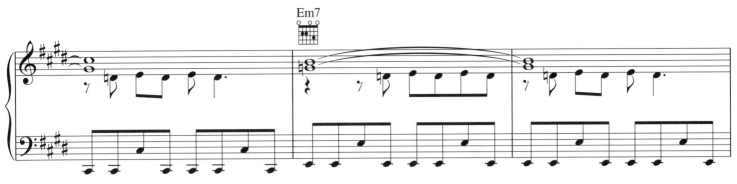

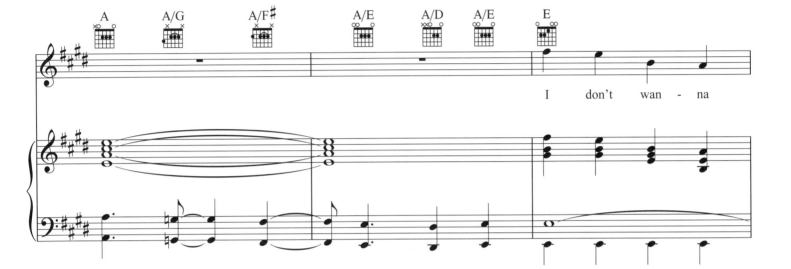

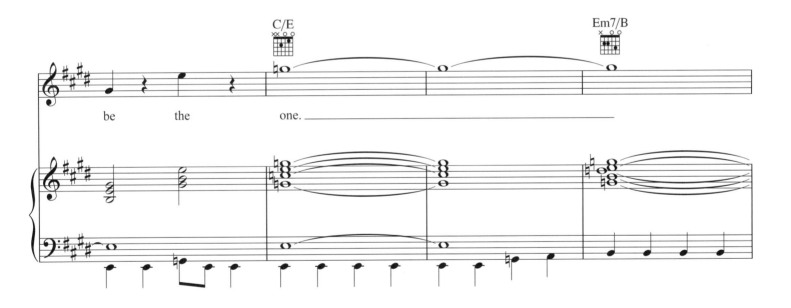

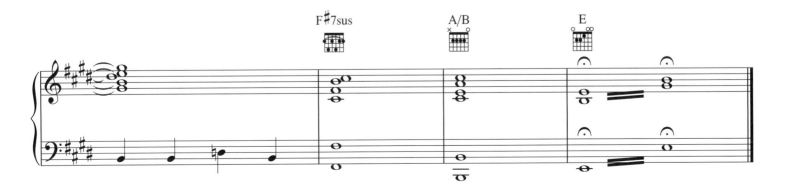

FORGOTTEN YEARS

Words and Music by ROBERT HIRST
and JAMES MOGINIE

Driving Rock

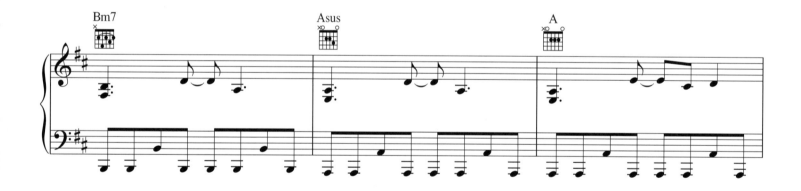

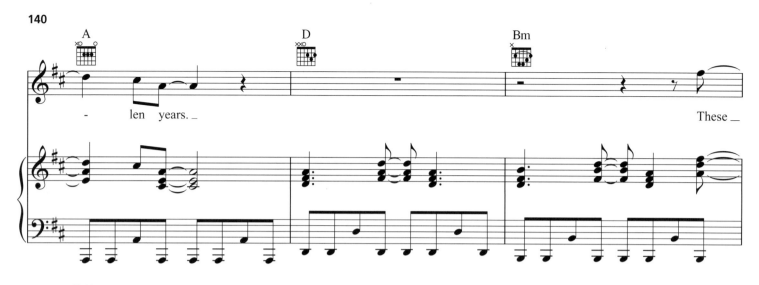

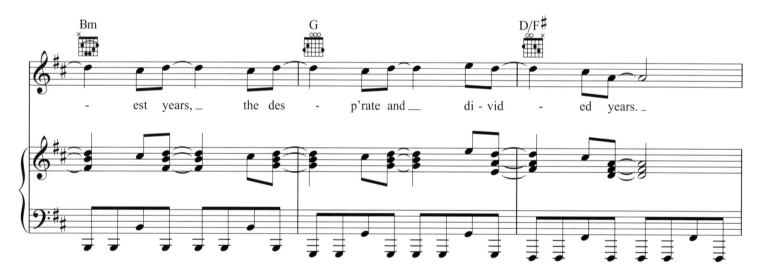

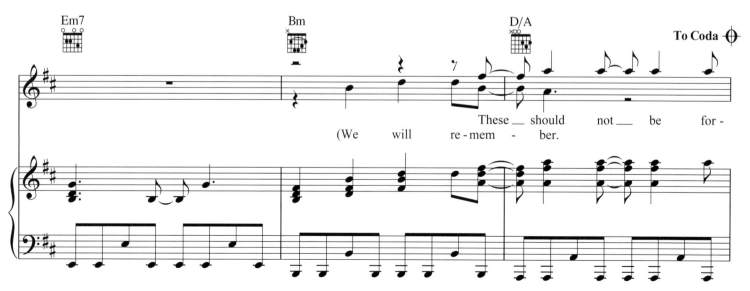

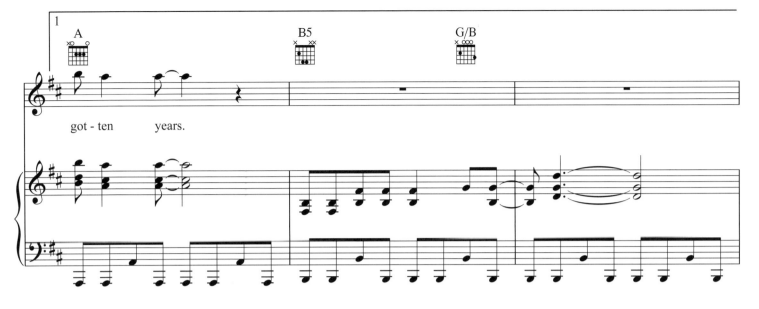

got - ten   years.

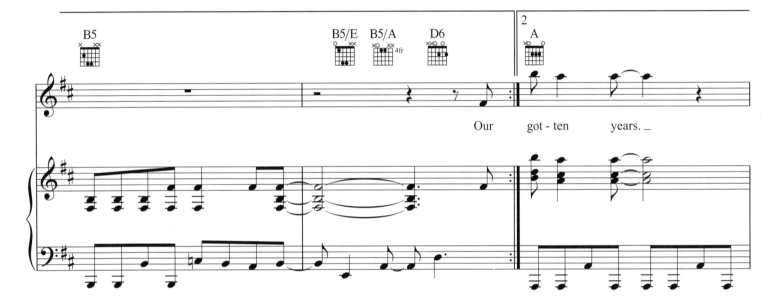

Our   got - ten   years. _

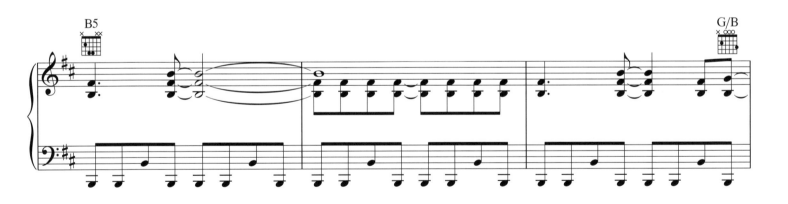

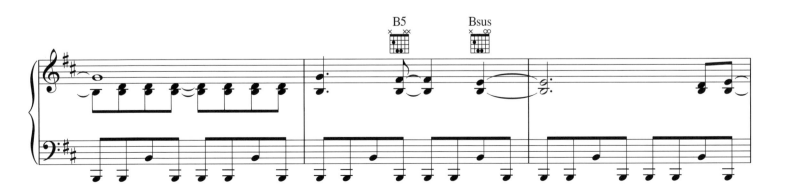

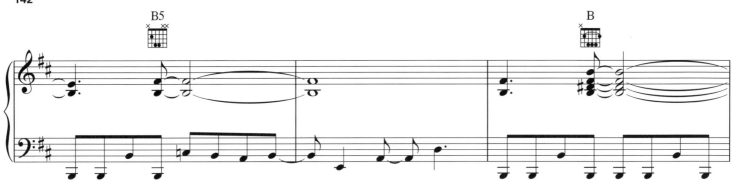

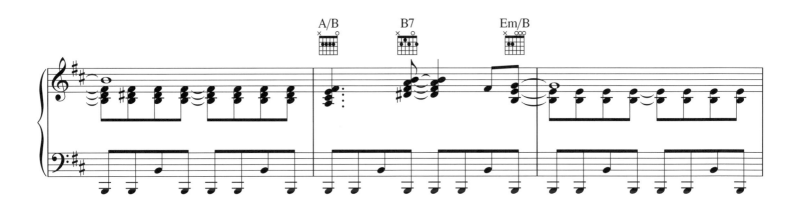

I said, __ it's the hard-

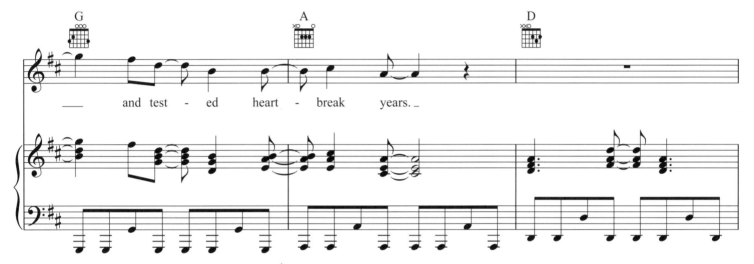

got-ten years. _ For-sak - ing, ach - ing, break - ing years. _ The time _

_ and test - ed heart - break years. _

Who needs your moth-er sing to you now! Oh, the blind -

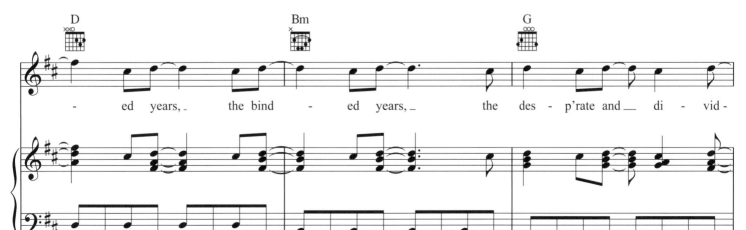

- ed years, _ the bind - ed years, _ the des - p'rate and _ di - vid -